ONE IN THIRTEEN
The Silent Epidemic of Teen Suicide

Jessica Portner
Foreword by Dr. William S. Pollack

Robins Lane Press
a division of Gryphon House, Inc.

Library of Congress Cataloging-in-Publication Data

Portner, Jessica, 1964-
      One in thirteen : The silent epidemic of teen suicide / by Jessica Portner.
        p. cm.
      Includes index.
      ISBN 1-58904-001-5
        1. Teenagers--Suicidal behavior--United States.   I. Title.
HV6546 .P67 2001
362.28'0835'0973--dc21   2001023470

Published by Robins Lane Press
A division of Gryphon House
10726 Tucker St., Beltsville, MD 20705 U.S.A.
Foreword copyright © 2001 by Dr. William S. Pollack
Appendix G - **Warning Signs** copyright © 2000
Community Health and Counseling Services of Bangor, Maine.
Reprinted with permission.
Printed in the United States of America
International Standard Book Number: 158904-001-5
01 02 03 04 05 06   15 14 13 12 11 10 9 8 7 6 5 4 3 2

ACKNOWLEDGEMENTS

FOR ALL THEIR HELP IN MAKING this book possible, I would like to thank: All of the families of the victims who agreed to speak with me and generously shared their personal stories, without whom this book would not have been possible; my editor and publisher at *Education Week*, Virginia Edwards, and *Education Week*'s Senior Editor Sandy Graziano for encouraging the original series of articles to be written and for giving me the time I needed to pursue it; my friend, *Education Week* Art Director Laura Baker, was also invaluable in helping me transfer the original articles into a book form; my wonderful editor at Robins Lane Press, Justin Rood, who worked so tirelessly and enthusiastically to make this book a reality; my dear friends Vicky Vogl, Rachel Neild, George McCabe, and Will Fleishell, for keeping me sane while writing about such a sad and complex subject; and finally, to my mother Dinah Berland and step-father Richard Garcia, both gifted poets, who taught me about the power of the written word.

CONTENTS

FOREWORD

"A lot of people use words like 'psycho' or 'wacko'
to refer to people who are feeling glum or think they
might want to take their own life. I think these sorts
of slang terms create further isolation in a teen, and
that's not what you want to do to a teen who already
feels alone."

—Gabe, age 18, from a small town in the South
From Real Boys' Voices (Random House, 2000)

SUICIDE AMONG ADOLESCENTS in our country is a major national crisis. Over the last fifty years the number of suicides among teens has risen dramatically; in fact, the suicide rate for adolescents has actually tripled since 1970. Yet in too many ways, the fact that suicide is the third largest cause of death for young people in this country often goes unnoticed. Teen suicide is an emotional cancer at the heart of our "successful society," but it has remained, for the most part, a hidden, *silent crisis*. Consequently, this major dilemma for American families, schools, children, and the entire fabric of our culture has remained almost completely unaddressed or inadequately responded to. This is especially troubling, when those of us who have studied, researched, and witnessed this pain I refer to as "self-murder" know it can be dramatically improved, if not eradicated.

I came upon this topic several years ago when I began my own research listening to "normal" boys' stifled voices of inner emotional pain. In my work, which led to the publication of *Real Boys*, I was struck by how many "boys next door," who seem just "fine," were beginning to tell me how they thought about taking their own lives. As I researched the data further, I found information not only about the rise in adolescent suicide, but also that boys, of various ages and ethnic backgrounds, were three to six times more likely to complete a suicide than girls! This was shocking not only because of the myth that boys are "hardy" while girls are the ones who get depressed, but also because I realized we were in the midst of a public health epidemic that was going unnoticed—while violence among male youth was blazoned across all our national headlines. That's when I came to hypothesize that as we raise our boys and girls in our society, we send them messages about "normalcy," which play a major role in murder and self-murder. I coined the phrase "Boy Code" to refer to the messages we often send our sons of stoicism and psychological repression that cut them off—particularly during their teenage years—from the human connections that they need to be genuinely emotionally healthy. That is why I believe there is a strong correlation between violence against others and violence directed toward the self—suicide or "self-murder."

Yet suicide is not only a dilemma for boys. The undiagnosed depression and suicidal enactment of girls has gone unnoticed, too. Girls, who "attempt" suicide four to six times more often than boys, are crying out for help, and yet, in so many instances, their cries are unanswered. Boys and girls are alike in the difficulties they face in garnering an appropriate response from the rest of society. In fact, in the ongoing Safe Schools Initiative of the U.S. Secret Service (in collaboration with the U.S. Department of Education) of which I am a consultant, we have found that many "school shooters" eventually confide their pain and plans in advance to a peer or adult, yet those confidants take no action before it is too late.

In addition to my own research and the research of others who have looked more closely into the deep emotional factors of teens' individual lives that either serve a protective function or leave them at risk, there is a growing body of statistical data (much of it summarized in The National Longitudinal Study on Adolescent Health, by Michael Resnick and his colleagues in "Protecting Adolescents from Harm") that speaks to those phenomena that best predict a teen's chances for an emotionally healthy trajectory of growth and protect against depression and suicide. Most striking is that of "perceived connectedness."

As Jessica Portner rightfully points out, there is no one clear cause for increased teen suicide, and no one magical program for the solution. Yet, a close reading reveals that when teens feel *connected*, especially to adults who understand and care about them, they will be less likely to become suicidal or, if depressed, more likely to reach out for help to those caring adults who have created for them what I call a "shame free zone." Indeed, the "empathic" school environments that Portner so feelingly describes are providing this emotional safety net for our teens.

The quotation with which I began this brief foreword comes from an interview for my book, *Real Boys' Voices*. Although I changed the name and geographical area to protect the teen's anonymity, these are his real words. His words speak to the centrality of the isolation and disconnection that can lead an adolescent to take his own life. As Jessica Portner describes, as adults we have cut off the lines of communication, stigmatized the pain of depression, and buried our heads in the sand.

My interview with this boy was striking because it brought me (much against my own wishes) into the midst of a potentially suicidal crisis—without a clear plan for action. Seeing teens in trouble is something I do every day in my clinical work, but here I was, a thousand miles from home in a strange city, with no connections and a potential crisis on my hands. I could empathize with the boys involved, as well as their parents and teachers, more than ever before. I was in the midst of the dilemma that Portner's book so eloquently describes.

Gabe, the boy quoted above, was not just speaking idly about teenage anomie. Instead, he was seeking help for his friend who I was going to interview in the next hour. He explained that his friend, Caleb, was becoming more and more "out of it" and depressed, but no one seemed to know what to do. His parents appeared to ignore it, the school saw it as a "slump" and gave him his space, and his friends caringly questioned him, only to be told what they knew in their hearts was untrue: "I'm okay . . . . I'm just having some bad days . . . it will get better." Gabe explained to me that he and his friends were worried that things were worsening, but didn't know who to go to for help. Now, they were reaching out to me. I suddenly felt an inner shudder in empathic resonance with their uncertainty. I was here as a researcher, not as a clinician. Certainly in an immediate emergency I could act, but short of that, what else could I do?

I waited with some trepidation for Caleb to arrive. When he arrived, I observed that he was slight of stature and somewhat taciturn with a downcast stare, but articulate and intelligent. Once I used my methods for making him feel emotionally safe, he was surprisingly open about his pain (to a point). He described a growing sense of depression, a fear of telling his parents because he thought they would be disappointed in him, a non-responsive interaction with a school guidance counselor, and friends who cared deeply, but whom he was afraid to tell the depth of his despair for fear of it "leaking" out to his whole school. I listened attentively, but quietly, and then asked, "Have you ever felt like taking your own life?"

Caleb was quiet for a long while. Then he sighed deeply and replied, "It's so obvious?"

"Yes and no," I replied. "Obviously, everyone close to you sees that things are going sour, but they are confused and afraid about the entire truth. I'm trained in this work, so it's a little clearer to me. But I think you want to reach out for help but don't know what to do."

He cried and we discussed alternatives. It would have been simple to just call the police and send him to a hospital, but if I did that, connection would not have happened among those who needed to achieve it. Caleb made clear that suicide was a significant issue, but not imminent. Therefore, I decided to try to create the safety net that Portner describes in this book. I told Caleb that his friends knew he was depressed and cared about him, so he needed to share with them, and I'd provide time for that after the interview. In addition, he needed to talk to his parents, and perhaps his friends could be part of that process. I also told him that he needed professional help, and the school had to link with him in a positive, supportive manner. We agreed that we would talk in three days (although I gave him a number to call at any time) and if by then the process wasn't going well, I'd step in to help. He agreed, and immediately seemed less anxious.

Two days later, I received calls from Gabe, Caleb, Caleb's parents, and the school principal. The parents were the most relieved. They told me, "We knew something was wrong for awhile, but we didn't know what to do! Then when Caleb came to us with his friends, even though the news was negative, we were almost relieved." Because his parents were far from disapproving, Caleb felt "a deeper connection" with them as they all arranged to see a mental health professional. His friends felt relief and began to work with the school principal to set up a suicide awareness and hotline program, co-run by students and faculty. Twenty students called for help in the first month.

Read *One in Thirteen* by Jessica Portner. If you are familiar with the silent crisis of teen suicide, it will cogently review the data and movingly tell the stories to renew your efforts to make change. If some or much of this is new to you, you will begin to look at the boy or girl in the seat in front of you, in the house next door, or in the room next to yours in a new and hopefully more connected way. You can make the difference between life and death. The time is now.

—WILLIAM S. POLLACK, PH.D.

Author of *Real Boys* and *Real Boys' Voices* and Director, Center for Men & Young Men at McLean Hospital; Assistant Clinical Professor, Department of Psychiatry, Harvard Medical School; Academic Advisor, President's Campaign Against Youth Violence; and Consultant, Safe Schools Initiative, U.S. Secret Service– Department of Education

PREFACE

THIS BOOK TOOK ROOT during the week of April 20, 1999, while I was holed up in a hotel room in Jefferson County, Colorado, covering a breaking story for *Education Week*, a weekly newspaper for educators. Like the throngs of media gathered there from around the world, my assignment was to report on the massacre in which two teenagers at Columbine High School shot and killed twelve classmates and a teacher and then shot themselves. I was struggling to write daily dispatches explaining how two affluent teenagers who lived in such a picture-perfect place could become so desensitized, so alienated, so ruthless.

People in that suburb of Denver seemed genuinely spooked that in their tranquil sanctuary in the Rocky Mountain foothills lurked a pair of adolescent monsters. But, of course, the teenage gunmen, Dylan Klebold and Eric Harris, were not mechanical toys whose insides could be easily disassembled and catalogued for display.

In addition to the challenge of explaining why the two dead teens had committed mass murder, I found myself in a unique predicament amid my journalist colleagues. As the crime reporter at *Education Week*, I was perhaps the only journalist in the country with a school crime beat. Because of my specialized approach, over the years I had already written many of the stories that led the news in the weeks following the tragedy: stories about which school safety techniques work and which don't, how kids gets guns, violence in the media, dress codes, how schools cope with tragedy. What I needed was a fresh angle.

Eventually, it struck me that, though this was a catastrophic homicide—and a huge news story—an even bigger story was being ignored. Everyone was focusing on the two boys as perpetrators, but, of course, they were also victims. And as I followed the stories of copycat suicides around the country, I was reminded that Klebold and Harris were not alone. Hundreds more children kill themselves than are killed at school—so many that U.S. Surgeon General David Satcher has called suicide America's hidden epidemic.

Despite its higher numbers, suicide tends to make headlines in national media only when it's a sensational mass suicide by a cult, or when a celebrity or politician takes his or her own life. A teenager's suicide might get a write-up in the hometown paper, but individual reports are usually so locally focused that they miss the insidious national phenomenon: The number of teen victims has been creeping up for years, and these children who are taking pills in their bedrooms or putting loaded guns to their heads are just like other children around the country who are poised to do the same.

Suicide has never spared the young, of course; but the pace has certainly quickened: Teen suicide rates in the

United States tripled between the 1960s and the 1990s. One in thirteen high school students attempts it each year.

For this book, I sought to gain a deeper understanding of those statistics—what they mean in human terms and what can be done to lower the casualty rate by taking away the means, motives, and opportunities.

To research the eleven-part *Education Week* series that was the basis for this book, I spent six months conducting more than a hundred interviews with families of victims, survivors of suicide attempts, educators, mental health policy experts, psychiatrists, epidemiologists, government researchers, and law enforcement officials. I also gathered and researched medical documents, police records, and school materials.

Many people I originally approached were understandably reluctant to discuss their personal experiences on the record. However, I was moved by the dozens of people who were willing to share their powerful stories with me. I am particularly grateful to the families of the three teenagers profiled in Part II for their candor and generosity.

As I sat in their living rooms, went to the schools these children attended, and listened to parents explain what it was like for them to lose a child, it was often a challenge to maintain a journalistic distance. Focusing on these tragedies for months on end often left me personally shaken—yet even more determined to write stories that would move people to pay attention to children at risk before it's too late.

Part I of this book explores the scope of the problem and the myriad reasons why young people commit suicide. It also looks at how they choose to die and at the differences in suicide rates between boys and girls, and among blacks,

Latinos, and whites. Part II profiles three children who committed suicide: a sixteen-year-old white boy from a suburb of Nashville, Tennessee; a black sixteen-year-old boy from Durham, North Carolina; and a thirteen-year-old Latina girl from Colorado Springs, Colorado. Each of the three stories shows the varied factors that can lead a child to commit such an act, and together they demonstrate that no single type of family, regardless of wealth or ethnic origin, is spared.

Part III takes a look at what is and isn't being done in the nation's schools and communities to address the problem. The lack of mental health support in schools and the paucity of training for school personnel are striking. Yet, as Part III shows, some schools and communities have come to the aid of the most vulnerable children, particularly gay youth, despite limited resources.

Although no one has a cure for suicide, and suicide will surely continue as long as humans suffer, the resources being assembled to reduce the rising numbers appear to be woefully inadequate.

In the grandest sense, I have come to see the rise in the youth suicide rate over the past thirty years as a kind of communal cry from the nation's youth for someone to "feel their pain," to rescue them from themselves, to give them a better way out. My hope is that this book makes their cries more audible.

—JESSICA PORTNER
Washington, D.C.

PART I. THE PROBLEM

Two TEENAGERS EXPLODED into their Colorado high school on April 20, 1999, and gunned down thirteen people, perpetrating the bloodiest school shooting in the nation's history. But nearly lost in the avalanche of reaction to the massacre at Columbine High School was the fact that the young men were also on a suicide mission.

The high school seniors had meticulously planned their own deaths—down to the last bullet and explosive—for nearly a year. They made pipe bombs at home and attached them to their bodies, apparently intending to blow themselves up along with the school. "They wanted to do as much damage as they possibly could and then go out in flames," John Stone, the Jefferson County, Colorado, sheriff, said that day.

But after the two boys had shot a dozen classmates, they discovered that the bombs they'd planted in the cafeteria had failed to detonate. So, instead, the teenagers used their back-up escape route: They turned their weapons on themselves and punched bullets into their own heads.

By committing mass murder, eighteen-year-old Eric Harris and seventeen-year-old Dylan Klebold joined a small group of other American teenagers. In their suicides, however, they had plenty of company.

For every adolescent who opened fire at schools from West Paducah, Kentucky, to Springfield, Oregon, in the late 1990s, thousands more shot themselves, slit their wrists, swerved their cars off embankments, or quietly gulped down lethal doses of pills in suicides or attempts. More American children are killing themselves today than at any other time in U.S. history.

To put this in perspective, eight students in the 1998–1999 school year committed homicides at school, and twenty-six students died violent deaths on school grounds. That same year, an estimated 2,700 young people ages ten to nineteen took their own lives.

Even more shocking than this youthful death toll is the fact that while American adults have been killing themselves less frequently, children keep beating their own record of self-destructiveness.

The number of thirty-, forty-, and fifty-somethings who take their own lives each year has steadied or even dropped over the past three decades. But since the 1960s, the suicide rate for teenagers has tripled.

"Where it used to be your grandfather, now it's your son," said Tom Simon, a suicide researcher at the U.S. Centers for Disease Control and Prevention (CDC).

In 1960, the suicide rate among fifteen- to nineteen-year-olds was 3.6 per 100,000. But by 1990, it was 11.1 per 100,000, according to the CDC. That means a school district with 100,000 students—about the size of Baltimore's—might expect eleven adolescents to kill themselves each year.

More American youth now die each year from suicide than from cancer, heart disease, AIDS, pneumonia, lung disease, and birth defects combined. For example, in 1996, more than 3,200 people under age 24 died of all those diseases, compared with more than 4,600 who took their own lives.

"This problem has reached epidemic proportions," said Richard Lieberman, a school psychologist with the Los Angeles public school system. "All across America, it is swept under the carpet. People are scared to face it."

LIKELY VICTIMS

Which teenagers are most likely to take their own lives? Is it the popular Romeo and Juliet couple who down a lethal concoction of barbiturates and alcohol after their parents bar them from seeing each other? Or is it the quiet, academically driven student whose parents are embroiled in a messy divorce who just snaps after failing a test? Or, in the stereotype of the Columbine killers, is it the rich, narcissistic nerd who plots an elaborate and public "escape" as a revenge against the world? The answer is all of the above.

No single group of children is exempt. Suicide does not discriminate by race, class, region, or gender. Upper-class urbanites, poor rural farm children, and middle-class kids crammed into minivans who become class presidents and get scholarships to Ivy League schools have all been victims of suicide.

However, in late twentieth century, particular groups of children have contributed to the unusual surge in the nation's youth suicide rate. Self-murder among preteens and young adolescents, aged ten to fourteen, has doubled since the 1960s. Also, black teenagers in the mid-1990s were more than twice as likely to kill themselves as they were a decade earlier. But white teenagers, particularly boys, still tower over their peers in their rates of self-destructiveness.

For every teenager who commits suicide, 100 more will try. Every year, one in thirteen high school students attempts suicide, a 1997 national survey found. Half of all high school students—or about 6 million kids—say that they have "seriously considered" suicide by the time they graduate, the survey reports.

That means in a class of forty students, three will attempt suicide and twenty more will seriously contemplate it. That's an estimated 700,000 American high school students who try to end it all each year—the equivalent of every student in the Los Angeles public schools.

Though teenagers commit suicide every day in rural communities, cities, and suburbs all across America, suicide rates have never been evenly distributed from state to state or region to region. New England has a much smaller percentage of teen suicides, while the western states, especially Montana, Colorado, Nevada, and Utah, consistently top the list. Some experts at the CDC blame the West's high rates on the relative social isolation of its residents. Some also have speculated that suicides are more common because those with a pioneering spirit who migrate west may be disappointed if they arrive at their destinations and their high expectations aren't met. If depression strikes, a psychologist may also be harder to find. Those sparsely populated states also tend to have fewer community institutions such as parks and fewer organized recreational activities to bring far-flung people together. "If people are moving all the time, those support systems may not be there and it may be harder to reach out and get help," one CDC researcher said.

Wherever they live, boys and girls tend to act very differently when it comes to planning and executing their own deaths.

While girls try to kill themselves three times as often as boys do, boys are four times more likely to finish the job. This gender gap reflects the fact that boys tend to employ more lethal means, such as firearms and hanging; girls favor more survivable methods, such as overdosing on pills. Roughly 23 percent of both male and female suicide victims hang or suffocate themselves. About 17 percent of teenage girls overdose on pills, a method chosen by only 4 percent of boys. Small percentages choose to die by drowning, in falls, or by slitting their wrists.

Girls attempt suicide more than boys, experts say, because their act is an effort at communicating their desperation. Boys tend to keep their emotions hidden. "Girls cry out for help, while boys are taught to be tough and never to 'act like a girl,'" said Dr. William S. Pollack, a psychologist and professor of psychiatry at Harvard Medical School and the author of *Real Boys: Rescuing Our Sons From the Myth of Boyhood.* As a result, Dr. Pollack said, "Boys are so ashamed of their feelings, they figure they'd be better off dead" than expressing their pain.

A small percentage of the increase in teenage suicide rates could reflect improvements in reporting over the past few decades, according to Lloyd Potter, an epidemiologist and suicide expert at the CDC. But, Mr. Potter said, rates have been and continue to be artificially low because suicides are often masked or misclassified.

A child's suicide is often camouflaged by parents who rearrange the site of the death or hide suicide notes. And some medical examiners classify a death as a suicide only when a note is found, something that occurs in less than a third of all cases.

"There's no doubt there are families who don't want it to appear on the death certificate, and the coroner obliges them," said Dr. Tom Shires, a trauma surgeon with the Suicide Prevention Research Center in Nevada. In some states, Dr. Shires added, the person designated to determine the cause of death may be a lawyer or a justice of the peace with no medical training who is ill-equipped to investigate such cases.

Dr. Shires, who is compiling a comprehensive database on suicide attempts among people of all ages, added that police are often complicit in the undercount of suicides. Law enforcement officers so consistently record single-car collisions as accidents that doctors have coined a term for them: autocides. Dr. Shires said the police file them away as accidents even when there are no skid marks on the pavement, which would indicate a desire to avoid a collision. Such misclassification throws off youth suicide rates because "unintentional injuries," primarily from automobile accidents, are the leading cause of death for fifteen- to nineteen-year-olds in the United States.

Another way suicide is hidden from the record books, say experts who study gangs, is that some teenagers who want to escape gang life but see no way out choose to die the "honorable" way by provoking police to fire at them.

"We call that 'suicide by cop,'" said Gloria Grenados, a psychiatric social worker at Bell High School in Los Angeles, a school whose students are nearly all affiliated with a gang, according to Grenados. "There are kids [who survived] who literally tell me they ran to meet the bullets because they so much wanted to die."

Taking note of such subterfuges, U.S. Surgeon General David Satcher called suicide "the nation's hidden epidemic." Suicide, Dr. Satcher said as he launched a suicide prevention campaign in the fall of 1999, must be destigmatized and addressed as a public health problem.

IMPULSIVE YOUTHS

Young people are more vulnerable than adults to thoughts of suicide, experts say, because they often don't comprehend in a rational sense that death is final. Suicide notes collected by researchers show children fantasizing about what they will do when they are dead. Young people often see suicide as the end of their problems, not their existence. "The developmental stage of adolescence is consistent with not thinking of the long- or short-term consequences of behavior," said the CDC's Mr. Simon.

Another tenet of child development is that adolescents are risk-takers by nature, who change friends, clothing styles, and attitudes constantly and for no apparent reason. Such impulsivity often rules when teenagers want to get rid of more than their wardrobes.

But impetuousness alone doesn't make a teenager suicidal, or virtually every teenager in the country would be a suicide risk. Things turn fatal when an adolescent's natural impulsivity is combined with environmental hazards such as abusive parents, vicious classmates, or a loaded gun under the bed.

The impetus for inner turmoil in the hearts of American adolescents in recent years cannot be gleaned from superficial clues such as whether a teenager plays violent video games, listens to Marilyn Manson CDs, or dons a black trench coat, school psychologists say. Young people rarely wear their angst so conveniently on their sleeves.

More often, they hide their pain from their parents, friends, and teachers by constructing elaborate disguises. Suicidal teenagers can act the part of well-adjusted children while their mind is consumed with planning their own deaths. One girl who attempted suicide as a teenager said she would plan the mechanics of her suicidal act in her head during family dinners. She said she'd have visions of leaping out a window, running in front of her school bus, or downing a handful of sleeping pills as her family quietly ate their roast chicken.

In his 1991 book *The Enigma of Suicide*, journalist George Howe Colt writes that searching for a single cause for suicide is as futile as "trying to pinpoint what causes us to fall in love or what causes war."

Finding an answer to the riddle of self-murder is not like tracing the origins of a disease to a single genetic marker. There is no one factor that causes suicide. Suicide is more like a multicolored tapestry that must be unraveled strand by strand to better understand how it happens and what can be done to thwart it.

Sociologists and mental health experts point to a tangle of cultural, psychological, and medical factors that have in the past thirty years fueled teenagers' heightened self-destructiveness: a higher divorce rate, parental abuse, poor impulse control stemming from exposure to television, the availability of handguns, lack of access to mental health services, and a general sense of isolation and alienation from caring adults both at home and at school.

Overall, the pressures—both in school and out—are weightier for kids today. There are fewer emotional buoys floating around for children to grab onto, so more of them plummet to the bottom, unless someone, somewhere, has taught them how to swim.

Some experts argue that the leading reason why young people are more at risk for suicide now than they were a generation or two ago is the decline of the traditional family unit.

The teenage suicide rate began its climb just as the divorce rate started to rise in the 1970s. Half of U.S. marriages now end in divorce, compared with 28 percent in the 1960s; 70 percent of children who attempt suicide have parents who are divorced. In addition, the percentage of children living with two parents declined from 85 percent in 1970 to 68 percent in 1996, federal statistics show.

The dissolution of a two-parent family, whether from divorce, desertion, or the death of a parent, makes children more vulnerable, experts say. A split, especially a rancorous one, divides children's loyalties and often makes them feel insecure just when they crave security most. Children of divorce, say psychologists, often blame themselves for their parents' problems.

Ultimately, though, it's the quality of the parenting, not the constitution of the family unit, that matters most, children's advocates say.

Whether married, divorced, or single, most parents are now working more than in the past and, as a result, have far less free time to spend with their children.

"We are benefiting in this society from everyone working, women working, productivity increasing," said Kevin Dwyer, past president of the National Association of School Psychologists (NASP). "But now kids are growing up without the supports they had in the past." The term "latchkey kid," for children left to fend for themselves at home after school, was coined in the 1980s. As on-the-job hours for most adults in the United States reached an all-time high in the 1980s and 1990s, alone time for kids has stacked up as well. Nearly 4 million children aged six to twelve who have working mothers don't have any adult supervision when they aren't in school.

To fill the parenting void and the decreasing ratio of caring adults to children, television increasingly has become children's stalwart companion after school. Parents spend an average of just two minutes a day communicating with their child, while the TV set spends an average of three and a half hours a day with that child, Mr. Colt writes in his book.

Study results are mixed on how exposure to media images of murders and assaults affects children's behavior, though many youth advocates are convinced that violent television shows, movies, and computer games inflame destructive tendencies. "Viewing violence can have lifelong harmful effects on children's health," according to the Center for Media Education (CME) in Washington, D.C. "The more violence they watch on television, the more likely they may act in aggressive ways, become less sensitive to others' pain and suffering, and be more fearful of the world around them."

More than 86 percent of television shows and movies depict characters who solve interpersonal problems with violence, according to NASP. The CME reports that by the end of elementary school, the average child will have witnessed more than 100,000 acts of violence on television, including 8,000 murders. Served the common fare of shootouts and knifings on TV, children come to believe that violence is an appropriate solution to problems, Mr. Dwyer said.

In today's media-saturated, high-velocity society, youths with poor impulse control are given the message that it's only natural that they should want everything yesterday.

While the video game industry rejects the idea that some of its games are virtual training classes for potential criminals, some recent, controversial studies contend that playing violent video games improves youths' dexterity with real firearms and desensitizes them to the visceral realities of violence. In one study from the late 1990s, high school students interviewed after suicide attempts expressed surprise that their actions were so painful, because it didn't look that way on TV.

The Media Factor

Some research suggests that the news media may foster children's self-destructive and violent behavior simply by reporting horrific events.

A 1986 study by Madelyn Gould, a professor of psychiatry at Columbia University who examined media coverage of suicides, found that the suicide of a person reported either on television or in newspapers makes at-risk individuals who are exposed to the coverage feel that suicide is a "reasonable, and even appealing, decision."

After the 1999 shootings at Columbine High School, which touched off weeks of intensive coverage by the national news media, there was a spike in teenage suicides across the nation, according to several experts. In Los Angeles County alone, six students killed themselves within six weeks of the shootings. In the four of those cases in which the students left notes, three mentioned Columbine as an inspiration. "If you plaster their face up on the news for twenty minutes, that's going to make the difference," said Harvard's Dr. Pollack. Media coverage of suicides isn't the reason children decide to kill themselves, Dr. Pollack said, but it is a contributing factor.

"These things open the floodgate," he said of news accounts. "But to flood, the waters have to already be at a high level."

Keeping afloat emotionally is challenging for many young people because the violence they're exposed to is not just on their television screens. Not surprisingly, children who suffer chronic physical or emotional abuse at home or who witness domestic violence are much more likely to kill themselves than their peers who do not witness such violence.

"A child doesn't just wake up suicidal," said Richard Lieberman, a school psychologist with the suicide prevention unit of the Los Angeles public schools who handles distress calls from school officials twenty-four hours a day. "Kids are dealing with more loss. Families are under more stress."

In all areas of the country—poor, rich, urban, suburban, and rural—reports of child abuse have accelerated dramatically in the past few decades. A small portion of the increase is attributable to better reporting; however, the bulk represents a real and disturbing trend, according to federal health officials. In 1997, 42 out of every 1,000 children in the United States were reported as victims of child abuse, a 320 percent leap from 10 per 1,000 children in 1976, figures from the U.S. Department of Health and Human Services show. Newspapers regularly report stories that were once rare: children locked in basements without food; battered and bruised toddlers entering shelters; teenage girls sexually assaulted by their fathers.

Changing School Climate

While home environments in general seem to have become more hazardous, so in large part have schools, say researchers who monitor the school climate. Apart from the increasing rates of assaults and shootings since the 1970s, garden-variety bullying behavior is rampant, says Dorothy Espelage, a professor of educational psychology at the University of Illinois at Urbana-Champaign. In a study published in 1999, Ms. Espelage found that 80 percent of 558 Illinois middle school students reported they had been "threatened, ridiculed, or been physically aggressive" with at least one classmate in the past thirty days. The bullying—which consisted of teasing, aggression, name calling, and social ridicule—was more often directed at children who appeared physically different in race or body size or who dressed differently than other kids. One in four children in the United States says they've been bullied at some point in their school careers, a separate study showed. Many children who are victimized by bullies retaliate and erupt into violence. Ms. Espelage says that 75 percent of the self-identified bullies in her study said they were targets of harassment themselves.

The class bully, of course, is as old as the classroom. But meanness seems to have become more sophisticated in recent years. It's easy to find Web sites these days where prepubescent hatemongers chat about their next target. "Many parents dismiss their children's fears as an inevitable part of school, but [bullying] can scar you in your mind more than physical abuse," and even lead to suicide, an official at Safe School/Safe Students, a national advocacy group, said.

Gay teens are particularly vulnerable to such taunting. A 1998 survey of 496 gay adolescents nationwide, commissioned by the Gay, Lesbian, and Straight Education Network, or GLSEN, found that 69 percent of gay students reported having been targets of verbal, physical, or sexual harassment in school and that 42 percent said they had been physically assaulted.

"It's a twenty-four-hour-a-day, seven-day-a-week saturation of antigay messages," said Rea Carey, executive director of the National Youth Advocacy Coalition, based in Washington, D.C. "If they hear messages day in and day out that say they are not of value to their community or their school, eventually those messages sink in."

Mark, a student at a high school in New York City, can testify to this. A shy 18-year-old, Mark downed a near-fatal dose of penicillin and painkillers in 1998. He could no longer endure the daily routine of being harassed at school—only to go home, where his brother beat him until he bled because he was gay. "I feel so unsupported," Mark said outside the New York City alternative school that he attends. "There's still some days I wish I were dead."

Homosexual youths are more than five times as likely to attempt suicide as their heterosexual peers. The taunts of "faggot" and "queer" that reverberate in school hallways, on street corners and playgrounds, and sometimes at the dinner table all combine to drive gay adolescents to the edge, said Ms. Carey.

Homosexual adults may have the emotional fortitude to deflect such ridicule, but adolescents typically are poorly equipped to repel jabs from their all-important peers. A 1991 University of Minnesota study found that the vast majority of suicide attempts by gay and lesbian adolescents were made within a year before or after they discovered their own sexual orientation.

While antigay harassment in school is a serious pressure on homosexual students, there are other school-related stresses that affect all students, gay or straight. The increasing drive toward raising academic performance has elevated many students' stress levels.

"We have become so focused on raising standards and testing students, and we are paying very little attention that this is working against creating a motivating environment for kids to come to school," said Howard Adelman, a professor of psychology at the University of California, Los Angeles (UCLA), who runs a project to promote mental health in schools.

Of course, not every student who feels pressured at school, is harassed, or has a chaotic home life becomes suicidal. A suicidal teenager is often fundamentally unstable, mental health experts say.

Currently in the United States, mental health experts say, an estimated 11 percent of children ages nine to seventeen—or 4 million children—have a diagnosable mental disorder, ranging from obsessive-compulsive disorder to major depression. The rate of depression has been rising among the young, researchers say, in part because the average age of puberty has declined and depressive illness tends to emerge after puberty.

Clinically depressed adolescents are five times more likely to attempt suicide than their nondepressed peers, according to a fifteen-year study that tracked seventy-three depressed adolescents and compared them with peers who were not clinically depressed.

Psychiatrists who have been enlisted to analyze the motivation of the Columbine shooters point out the fact that Eric Harris was being treated with an antidepressant. The teenager was in psychotherapy and was known to have taken a prescription medication used to treat obsessive-compulsive disorder. Some psychiatrists have suggested that certain drugs used to treat depression, bipolar disorder (also called manic depression), and other mood disorders might actually provoke psychosis in a small percentage of patients. An estimated 3 percent of adults taking certain psychiatric medications have had psychotic reactions that include bouts of violence and delusional episodes. While most antidepressants have yet to be tested on people under eighteen, some researchers suggest these reactions could be as much as two to three times higher in children. But psychologists say that, in the vast majority of cases, it is unlikely that violent attacks happen just because a child swallowed a pill. More often, mental health experts say, things go haywire when children *don't* get the medical and therapeutic help they need to sort through their emotional pain.

In her book, *Night Falls Fast: Understanding Suicide*, Dr. Kay Redfield Jamison, a professor of psychiatry at Johns Hopkins University, says clinical depression is quite distinguishable from common adolescent angst. "In its severe forms, depression paralyzes all of the otherwise vital forces that make us human, leaving instead a bleak, fatiguing, deadened state," she writes.

In *Darkness Visible*, author William Styron describes his own severe depression as "a hurricane of the mind." And five years before killing herself, poet Sylvia Plath said of her depressive moods, "I felt as if I were smothering. As if a great muscular owl were sitting on my chest, its talons clenching and constricting my heart."

A growing number of children are now being treated for mood disorders. In 1996, 600,000 children under age eighteen with clinical depression were prescribed the anti-depressants Prozac, Paxil, and Zoloft, according to IMS America, a research group in New York City. Because no groups have conducted long-term studies on children's use of antidepressants, it is difficult to determine whether such medicinal remedies can lift the suffocating darkness that Dr. Jamison describes.

Whatever the effect, the upsurge in prescribing psychiatric medications has occurred mainly in middle- and upper-class populations, in which children have more access to health care. For millions of teenagers in less fortunate circumstances, the last trip to any kind of doctor was for childhood inoculations.

A 1999 study by the University of North Carolina at Chapel Hill found that one-fifth of teenagers said they had received no professional health care in the past six months, even though they had a condition that warranted a medical visit. That situation represents a lost opportunity, suicide experts say, because family doctors can detect sudden changes in mood, sleeping patterns, and eating habits—all indicators of depression. A patient who goes to the doctor complaining of asthma or insomnia might actually have a more fatal condition. But suicidal thoughts aren't detectable with stethoscopes or brain scans; it takes a more subtle approach, says Dr. Shires.

Some depressed teenagers who are either embarrassed to seek help or can't afford it eschew traditional medical care in favor of illicit drugs to elevate their moods. There is a strong link between the use of illicit drugs and suicide; alcohol and certain drugs are depressants and often deepen a depressed mood. And, because they knock down inhibitions, they make teenagers feel freer to act on their suicidal fantasies.

Autopsies of adolescent suicide victims show that one-third to one-half of them were under the influence of drugs or alcohol shortly before they killed themselves, according to statistics from the Department of Health and Human Services. The overall rate of teenage drug use has fluctuated over the past three decades, peaking in the 1970s and then receding somewhat in the 1980s. Use of marijuana and alcohol—both depressants—surged in the 1990s.

While teenage attendance at religious services rose in the late 1990s, far fewer adolescents attend than did twenty years ago. Religious affiliation as a buffer against the harsh realities of the world has a solid grounding in research. For example, studies have shown that elderly people who participate in church-based activities—such as social events and bingo games—have a decreased risk of mortality. A 1998 study published in the *Southern Medical Journal* found that elderly people who attended church every week and who said God was a source of comfort in their lives recovered faster from depression than those who didn't attend religious services. However, researchers say that better mental health could be due as much to the balm of faith as to the fact that attending places of worship decreases isolation.

MEANS AND REASONS

The burgeoning numbers of isolated, despondent teenagers now more than ever have lethal means at their fingertips.

The federal Bureau of Alcohol, Tobacco, and Firearms (ATF) reports that in 1960, 90 million guns were in circulation; in 1999, an estimated 200 million firearms were in private hands. That's enough weaponry, if distributed among the U.S. population, to arm three out of four Americans. Despite state and federal laws banning possession of handguns by anyone under eighteen, many young people know that getting a firearm is no more complicated than pilfering from a parent's closet. The ATF, which traces gun purchasing patterns, says minors usually get handguns in one of three ways: by borrowing, stealing, or buying them illegally. In almost any big city and in many small towns in America, a resourceful teenager can, with a little research, find out where to buy guns, ATF officials say. Smith & Wessons, Glocks, various rifles, and shotguns can sell for as little as $20—a few days' lunch money—on the street.

In December 1993, sixteen-year-old Aron Gilliam went to the corner of Jefferson and 33rd in downtown Savannah, Georgia, and bought a .32 caliber revolver from a crack dealer for $20. A few days later Gilliam used the weapon to kill a classmate on the steps of his school. "Anywhere you have crackheads, there's going to be guns," said Brett Tremelling, a narcotics officer in a suburban Savannah police department who confiscates an average of three guns every time he goes on a drug raid.

A smaller number of minors steal guns by burglarizing gun dealers or pawnshops. A pawnshop owner in Savannah said that the number one reason his store is vandalized is for guns. Most of the time, however, children who are looking for firearms find them at home.

Access is key when you consider that guns are the overwhelming method of choice for suicidal youths: More than

67 percent of boys and nearly 52 percent of girls ages ten to nineteen who kill themselves use a firearm.

Before a youth pulls the trigger, experts say, some event usually has to set him or her off. A recent survey of fifteen- to nineteen-year-old students in Oregon who had attempted suicide found that the top three things that spurred them to act—while none was the sole reason—were conflicts with parents, relationship problems, and difficulties at school.

Whatever the eventual catalyst, every suicidal youth's life story has a uniquely tragic plot. More often than not, it's a circuitous route that leads him or her toward suicide.

Most children who take their own lives don't wake up the morning of their deaths with the means, motive, and opportunity sketched out neatly in their heads. Many teenagers who have survived suicide attempts said they did it because of a pain, slight, or shame they could no longer bear. They say at the time they felt as if they were enveloped in a haze, lost in the center of a raging tornado, all alone and unable to conceive that this terrifying moment would ever end—unless they did something to stop it.

It's tempting to see suicidal intent as an invisible virus attacking the host's immune system, breaking down the body's defenses until its victim is leveled by some opportunistic infection, an environmental blow. But the reason there is no one cure for suicide is because there is no one cause. In each sorrowful scenario, a peculiar combination of character traits, circumstances, and events conspired to usher one person to an early death.

The stories of the teenagers in the following section show this all too well.

PART II. DYING YOUNG

Jason Flatt, 1981–1997

JASON FLATT WAS THE last student in Good Pasture High School's class of 2000 that anyone expected to shoot himself in the head.

When he killed himself in 1997 at age sixteen, Jason, the son of an insurance executive and a hospital worker, was a promising freshman football player who earned decent grades at the private Christian schools he had attended since sixth grade.

Hendersonville, Tennessee, the suburb of Nashville where Jason grew up, is a Capra-esque community of 36,000 where most teenagers would sooner go to church youth groups than raves and where parents make time in their loaded professional schedules to help their children decorate crepe-paper floats for the homecoming parade.

The only signs of bustle in this languid town are the ubiquitous chocolate-colored tour buses loading up local country bands for road trips or ushering tourists to the Grand Ole Opry.

Jason Flatt fit in here. When he was younger, the gregarious boy with a sly grin was never without a companion. "Other kids wanted to be on his team," said Beverly Moore, his seventh grade English teacher.

Jason's older brother John, who eventually went to medical school at the University of Tennessee, Memphis, was always the academic heavyweight in the family. John was the president of the honor society at Davidson Academy, the private K–8 school he and Jason had attended, and he graduated in the top of his class at Good Pasture. Jason was a solid B student throughout school, but comparisons to his brother never seemed to dull his playful mood.

"Jason was an intelligent, fine student. But it was like, 'Why worry about an A when you can get a B and have a lot of fun?'" Ms. Moore said.

It was Jason's artistic predilections that Sharon Bracy, his seventh grade science teacher, remembers. At age eleven, Jason would neatly arrange specimens in a scrapbook after class outings to collect dandelions, chickweed, and mint. While other students scribbled in cell biology class, Jason took his time sketching detailed pictures of amoebas and paramecia.

When Jason went on to Good Pasture for high school, he quickly became a fierce competitor on the football team. What the freshman running back lacked in stature—he was five feet, nine inches and weighed 174 pounds in a field of bulky giants—he made up in heart. "He wasn't big, but he was tough and smart and had good speed," said coach David Martin, who remembers Jason running sixty yards for a touchdown the year the Cougars were runners-up in the state championship.

Off the field, Jason eschewed drugs and alcohol for wholesome amusements such as roller coaster rides and water sports.

At Anchor High Marina, where he worked during the summer pumping gas for the phalanx of motorboats that buzzed along Old Hickory Lake, his bosses describe him as an industrious employee.

"He was a good, all-American boy who was willing to work," Billy Etheridge, the marina's manager, said as he toiled over the engine of a speedboat under the shade of a maple tree. "If I told him to empty Old Hickory Lake, Jason would come down and start pumping the water."

"Jason was one of the most personable, happy, cheerful kids I saw in my life," said Art Merridink, the principal of Davidson Academy.

On July 16, 1997, that wasn't the case. Jason Flatt drew straws with his brother John in the morning over who would pump gas at the marina that sticky midsummer day. The younger brother begged off, saying he wanted to take a spin with a friend on the family's boat, the *Sea Doo*. Later that afternoon, another friend called Jason's father at his office to tell him that Jason had canceled the outing and seemed angry about something. Clark Flatt paged his son repeatedly and became concerned when the conscientious boy didn't respond.

Mr. Flatt drove all over town trying to spot his son's car. "I wanted to find him; I thought we could get a Coca-Cola and talk about what's going on," Mr. Flatt said. When he saw his son's car in the driveway at home, he was relieved.

He walked through the house calling Jason's name, but there was no reply. Mr. Flatt recalls that their usually affectionate dog, Holly, was strangely huddled in a corner, and that a bright light was shining in Jason's bedroom. When Mr. Flatt pushed the door open, he literally tripped over his son's blood-soaked body.

Jason Flatt was dead from a self-inflicted gunshot wound to the head. A stainless-steel .38-caliber pistol lay on the floor.

"It never crossed my mind that [Jason] would hurt himself," Mr. Flatt, said from his office in 1999. "Why didn't I know what was happening to my son?"

As mysterious as suicide is, Jason Flatt's death is even more incomprehensible to his family and friends because the teenager didn't fit the traditional profile of the alienated loner with a serious mental illness or the low-achieving student with a drug problem.

But in the cold statistical calculus of age and race and gender, Jason Flatt's face is the face of teenage suicide. White males in their late teens have the highest youth suicide rate of either gender or any racial group. According to the CDC, nearly 16 out of every 100,000 fifteen- to nineteen-year-old white males committed suicide in 1997.

What Jason's story reveals is a frightening truth: Seemingly well-adjusted teenagers, particularly boys who may see few emotional outlets for their pain, may need only access to a gun and a single traumatic event to give in to a self-destructive impulse.

For Jason Flatt, the catalyst was a girl. According to Hendersonville police reports, Jason killed himself less than twenty-four hours after his girlfriend ended a tumultuous three-month relationship. The two had been planning to drive to Albany, New York, together for a rendezvous, the girl told police, but she canceled the plans at the last minute.

Shayne Nolan, one of Jason's best friends and football buddies, maintained that the girl had been spreading false stories about the couple. On the practice field at Good Pasture High during a break between plays, Shayne shook his head. "She messed with his mind," he said.

Coach Martin, sitting in his field office papered with photos of the Cougars' winning teams, used a sports analogy to explain the tragedy: "Jason had a competitive spirit, and if you challenged him he was going to respond," he said, looking up at a picture of the championship 1996 junior varsity team that shows Jason with a tough-as-a-bulldog stare. "True athletes' will to win is so great that they don't deal well with situations where they can't win. In this situation [with his girlfriend], maybe he felt he just couldn't win."

The sense of loss that Jason Flatt felt when a girl broke up with him was so crushing probably because he—like many other adolescent boys—felt uncomfortable expressing his feelings in the first place, said Harvard's Dr. Pollack.

More than 85 percent of completed teenage suicides in the United States are by boys, and nearly all teenage murderers are male.

Social science studies have shown that boys aren't more genetically predisposed than girls to be aggressive or violent, but from early childhood, boys are more likely to be taught a "boy code" in which they are discouraged from discussing their emotions and are steered instead toward physical outlets, said Dr. Pollack, the author of *Real Boys*.

Studies of families with small children have shown that, from infancy, baby boys are often prodded to dry their tears, while baby girls are coddled.

Mike Settle, a coach and Bible-study teacher at Davidson Academy who often traveled with Jason Flatt to out-of-town games, said he sees the effect of those gender roles every day. "In a country where John Wayne leads by example, guys are reluctant to talk," he said. "Girls are open, but guys, when I call them into my office, often just shrug and grunt and turn inward."

While Jason assumed a strong-guy stance and often hid behind a happy-go-lucky mask, the teenager's ebullient demeanor was occasionally punctuated by rage, his family and friends say.

Less than a year before his death, for example, Jason got "shaking angry" when he was told he couldn't borrow the car, according to his father. "He went from an even keel to uncontrolled anger," Mr. Flatt said.

But those temporary flare-ups were never so profound or noticeable that they warranted professional psychiatric intervention. To his parents and friends, Jason's moodiness was garden-variety adolescent angst.

Through a controversial method of posthumous diagnosis, a psychiatrist friend of Mr. Flatt's said he saw indications that Jason could have suffered from bipolar disorder. But that psychiatrist and other mental health professionals say Jason provided too little evidence to make any firm diagnosis.

Looking back, Coach Martin recalled that Jason's grades had slipped to Cs in the weeks before his death. And some of Jason's friends remember that he made offhand remarks about quitting football during the same time.

"He was losing interest all at once," his father said.

Still, Matt Hart, Jason's best friend and the quarterback of the Cougars football team, doubts that he had been actively planning to end his own life. He left no note, no written declaration, Matt said, after football practice in fall 1999. "If he'd thought about what he was doing, he wouldn't have done it. He was smarter than that."

Such impulsivity—whether self-destructive or not—is a basic trait of many adolescents.

"In general, in the developmental stage, kids are trying lifestyles on constantly, so there is greater risk-taking," said Mr. Simon of the CDC. Teenagers may switch personas as often as they do hairstyles.

That quickness in making decisions is one reason why the suicide rate among adolescents is higher than that of almost any other age group, said Mr. Simon, who has studied the extent of impulsivity in suicidal teenagers.

Preliminary results from the study found that 50 percent of suicide survivors said they had been thinking of suicide for less than twenty-four hours—or, in many cases, a matter of minutes—before they made an attempt.

In a separate CDC-financed study, researchers interviewed 153 thirteen- to thirty-four-year-olds in Houston who had survived a suicide attempt between 1992 and 1995. The study found that for one-quarter of the group, less than five minutes had passed between the time they decided to commit suicide and the time they swallowed the pills, slit their wrists, or shot themselves.

Older suicide survivors, in contrast, often said they had spent months planning their deaths, sometimes writing their wills and making funeral arrangements.

John Flatt said he has spent the past two years wondering what prompted his younger brother—and not him—to take that fatal step.

"A lot of us have been to the point where suicide pops in your head," he said. "But if we are cognitive enough, we are frightened by our thoughts of killing ourselves, and there's a trigger that scares you for even thinking of ending your life. For Jason, that check mechanism didn't work."

Still, Jason might not have succeeded in acting on his impulse if he hadn't picked up his father's gun.

Though firearms have always been present in many American households, federal statistics suggest that self-destructive teenagers are more likely than ever to have such lethal means at their disposal.

Federal Bureau of Investigation reports show that 100 million guns have come into circulation in the United States in the past two decades. In 1970, guns were used by fewer than half of all suicide victims ages fifteen to twenty-four; by 1990, the proportion had risen to two-thirds.

Minors generally acquire weapons in one of three ways: They buy them illegally, borrow them from a relative, or steal them from places such as pawnshops. Currently, 51 percent of American households report keeping a gun at home. The vast majority of the minors who use guns to kill themselves or others snatch the weapons from a cabinet or drawer in the house.

"Jason never cared for guns," Mr. Flatt said, recalling how his son had recoiled when he first showed him the Smith & Wesson that he kept in his closet for protection. Mr. Flatt said Jason had never even cocked the trigger of a gun before he turned one on himself.

"I had it in my bedroom, always loaded in case of burglary," Mr. Flatt, who is a now a staunch advocate of trigger locks, said of the pistol his son used. An $8 safety device could have saved Jason's life, he said.

In their new brick house across town, with a modest, manicured lawn and a tidy ring of pink flowers, Clark and

Connie Flatt keep their memories of Jason in a box: a phone their mechanically inclined son dismantled and reassembled, a photo album, a picture of him smiling at a birthday bash, neatly folded letters to friends.

Beyond those keepsakes, Jason's father has sought to preserve Jason's memory through a foundation he started months after his son's death.

The Jason Foundation teaches young people through its suicide prevention curriculum to speak up when a friend even fantasizes about ending it all. In 70 percent of all teenage suicides, another teenager knew about the victim's intentions beforehand, according to foundation literature.

In its first two years, the Jason Foundation has distributed its curriculum, financed by Mr. Flatt's insurance business, to schools in twenty-eight states.

"We tell them, 'Watch your brother and sister,'" Mr. Flatt said. "We aren't trying to make counselors out of fifteen-year-olds. We just want them to extend a hand."

MEKYE MALCOLM, 1981–1998

Classmates used to call him "Houdini" for the way he would deftly slip out of class and wander the hills behind his school, sketching pictures of butterflies and horses nipping at the green North Carolina grass.

So Mekye Malcolm's fellow students at Carolina Friends School in Durham weren't all that surprised on the cloudy afternoon of April 14, 1998, when the sixteen-year-old freshman was missing from his fifth-period science class.

Administrators at the 490-student private school on the outskirts of this university town were deeply worried,

however. They knew Mekye Malcolm was emotionally troubled, and they had allowed him to return to school after a
suicide attempt a few months earlier on the condition that
everyone would keep an extra-close watch on his where-
abouts.

While teachers scoured the thirty-five-acre wooded
campus looking for the missing teenager, Mekye was on the
baseball field, setting a chair under a sourwood tree behind
the third-base dugout. There he would have a lovely view of
the flower-dappled hillside. But this time, he didn't go there
to draw.

He positioned the chair under a low-lying branch that
held a nylon rope used for wiffle-ball practice, cinched the
cord tight around his neck, then crouched down, holding his
knees inches from the ground and choking off his own
breath.

Jim Henderson, the head high school teacher at the
K–12 school, found Mekye Malcolm that afternoon, with
his knees skirting the dirt and head bowed forward, "just
as if he were praying."

"There was literally just enough rope to hang himself
with," and it was just strong enough to hold his large frame,
Mr. Henderson said. Mekye had had time, perhaps several
minutes, to change his mind.

"He was a loner. He never really talked to friends on
the phone. It used to worry me," said his half-brother John
Watkins, who is ten years older than Mekye.

During Mekye's childhood, the family moved throughout the South as his mother, Nayo Watkins, an arts educator and playwright, followed her husbands and chased her
own job opportunities.

Ms. Watkins' seven children came from three different marriages. She never married Mekye's father. It seemed the only thing Mekye Malcolm ever received from his biological father was his name.

Ms. Watkins and her second husband, Hollis Watkins, Sr., divorced before Mekye was even born, but Mr. Watkins was a surrogate father for the boy throughout his childhood. A former civil rights leader from Mississippi, Mr. Watkins would regale Mekye with stories of how he used to sign up blacks to vote during the 1960s. After Ms. Watkins moved her family to North Carolina in 1990 to take a job as an administrator for a dance company, Mr. Watkins' visits became more sporadic.

During that period, Mekye's longing for his absent biological father started to sting, his friends at school say. "He was angry at his [biological father] who left him, and he felt like he was in limbo," his friend Hilary McKean-Peraza recalled.

A few years after moving to North Carolina, brothers John Watkins and Hollis Watkins, Jr.—seven years older than Mekye and closest to his age—both left for college, leaving the baby of the family essentially an only child.

Mekye also started to feel increasingly alone in the Durham public schools. By fifth grade, he was having difficulty with even basic tasks that required short-term memory, such as keeping track of homework assignments. Mekye eventually was diagnosed with dyslexia and attention deficit disorder, and Ms. Watkins transferred him to Carolina Friends School fifteen miles from their home.

For a single mother earning $35,000 a year with two sons in college, it was a financial hardship to scrape up the $6,000 a year for tuition to send Mekye to private school. But Ms. Watkins applied for and received a federal grant to help low-income, self-employed families and scrimped. "I did the best I could," she said, "but I stayed in the red."

When he entered the sixth grade at Carolina Friends School, Mekye finally started to progress. Nancy Parsifal, a middle school teacher, said that when she first saw Mekye, he was sitting at a table crying because he could barely read.

For the next three years, Ms. Parsifal and the other teachers drilled him on reading skills and taught him math using visual objects rather than requiring calculations in writing. Children who have dyslexia, a problem in the brain's language center, have difficulty recognizing individual syllables of words—the necessary building blocks for reading.

Mekye made progress in seventh and eighth grades. But when he made the leap to ninth grade, with more academically rigorous courses and less individualized instruction, he hit a wall.

As the inevitable cliques of high school developed, Mekye also became more aware of how, as an African American, he was set apart from his peers: He was one of only eleven black students in the high school. Most of his classmates were from affluent suburban families, while he came from modest circumstances and lived in the city.

"This was a private school of kids who have means. Mekye was aware that these kids lived in different neighborhoods that had different furniture," Ms. Watkins said. Though the school took pains to be inclusive, such as observing Black History Month, Ms. Watkins said, "It was still like, 'We want your little colored face in the circle while we do our Eurocentric thing.'"

Soon, Mekye started getting into mischief. After school, with his neighborhood friend Daniel Hogan, he would pop streetlights with a BB gun, and once the two of them started a fire in the middle of their street using brambles, alcohol, and leaves.

During that time, Daniel said, he and Mekye tried marijuana a couple of times and started drinking beer. But the two boys never talked about emotional problems, so Daniel was surprised when he heard that his friend had barricaded himself in his bedroom and slashed his wrists. When the police came to break down the door, they found that Mekye, who had asthma, had also activated a fire extinguisher, which could have sent him into a fatal asthmatic shock. He was hospitalized at Duke University Medical Center for a week, then discharged with a prescription for the antidepressant Zoloft.

Nothing, though, seemed to help his mood. His mother said he was like a walking pharmaceutical experiment, testing out several prescription drugs in a matter of weeks.

Earlier on the morning of Mekye's death, the mellow, camplike atmosphere of his school was shattered by a girl's scream. Mekye's friend Hilary, whom he apparently had a crush on, had suffered a postoperative muscle cramp in class that required immediate medical attention.

Mekye helped her into her mother's van, but Hilary's boyfriend rode with her to the hospital. As the van pulled away, Mekye started crying. Tom Lamanna, a classmate who went over to comfort him, said that Mekye was mumbling that he had somehow caused the girl's injury. "He cried for a few minutes, and then asked me to leave," Tom remembered. "Then he walked away up to the field."

Later, the police found a picture Mekye had drawn in art class that morning: It was an admirable rendering of a tree branch and a rope.

Ms. Watkins doesn't like the image of a young black man hanging from a tree because of what it inevitably conjures up: "Lynchings bring horror to one's heart."

In many ways, Mekye Malcolm suffered from the same societal pressures that experts suggest are driving more black teenage boys to end their lives.

The suicide rate for black teenagers has more than doubled in the past two decades. The rate of suicides among black male teenagers increased from 3.6 per 100,000 in 1980 to 8.1 per 100,000 in 1995, according to a recent study by the CDC. And the numbers have continued to rise.

Social scientists say one reason for the dramatic increase in the black teenage suicide rate may be that as more black families make the transition into the middle class, community and family networks are splintering.

"As African Americans move into the middle class and are isolated more from their community, there's no comfort zone," said Donna Holland Barnes, a professor of sociology at Southwest Texas State University. Ms. Barnes, who founded the National Organization of People of Color Against Suicide after her son killed himself, said that many of the youngsters who straddle two worlds the way Mekye Malcolm did feel the pressure of trying to compete in a white-dominated society.

Les Franklin, whose fifteen-year-old son committed suicide recently, now runs an organization for African-

American youths. He said black teenagers lack the social support that existed in earlier decades. The solidarity of the civil rights era provided young people with a support network with which to battle the overt racism of the time.

"These kids today aren't fortified to deal with the subtle discrimination like I was," Mr. Franklin said. "They give in to things my generation would resist."

The lack of access to mental health services in many black communities might also be a factor driving black youths to suicide, said Tonji Durant, an epidemiologist at the CDC and the author of a study on black teenage suicide. More than a quarter of all adolescents lack a regular source of health care, and many health insurance plans don't include coverage for mental health care, she said.

In addition to a paucity of services, many in the black community have an inherent distrust of the mental health care system, Ms. Durant said. "For many blacks," she said, "seeking mental health care is a sign of weakness. They just say, 'go pray.'"

Nayo Watkins, Mekye Malcolm's mother, agrees that blacks' pride in their self-reliance at overcoming adversity runs deep. "We came here on slave ships. We didn't jump off," she said. "Even in the face of the worst, we have a spiritual sense of making it to the next day."

"Blacks think of suicide as a character flaw," Ms. Barnes added. "In other communities, it's an illness."

Even when she brought her son to the hospital after his first suicide attempt, Ms. Watkins hadn't fully registered what was happening to him. She said she didn't understand depression as a serious medical condition. "The nurse told me he had depression, and I thought, 'I've pulled a lot of folks through bad times,'" she said. "I didn't know the difference between clinical depression and having a bad day."

Since her son's death, Ms. Watkins has learned that depression like his can be worsened by such stresses as chronic failure at school.

Children with learning disabilities are nearly twice as likely as nondisabled children to experience serious bouts of depression that could lead to suicide, according to William N. Bender, a professor of special education at the University of Georgia, who reviewed the literature on learning disabilities and self-destructive behavior for a 1999 study.

Andrew Short, a Durham psychologist who treated Mekye's dyslexia, said the boy's problems in school were a catalyst for his depression. "School is the main arena they perform in, and if kids aren't successful, that bothers them," he said.

Mekye had struggled to bring his academic skills in line with his intellectual ability, but his teachers saw his effort lag as his progress slowed in ninth grade.

John Baird, the principal of Carolina Friends School, said officials there made many attempts to accommodate Mekye's difficulties with reading and writing by personalizing assignments and requiring less written work. In social studies, for example, Mekye studied history through film.

"We did all we could to meet his needs," Mr. Baird said from his office at the school.

Mr. Henderson, the head high school teacher, added, "Mekye's problems were of a magnitude we weren't able to deal with."

Ms. Watkins, however, thinks the school didn't do everything it reasonably could have to help her son academically or emotionally. When his injured friend left school and Mekye sat on a bench crying, an adult should have intervened, his mother said. "Here is a child with a mental ailment who was crying, and they left him alone," she said. "What would they have done if the child had a physical ailment? They would not have left him." Her son's death, Ms. Watkins said, was "a tragedy of errors."

In a corner of her living room, Nayo Watkins keeps a cluttered shrine to her dead son: a professional-looking wooden pencil box that he carved by hand, several unfinished charcoal portraits, his wooden walking stick, and his size 16 Nikes.

Over the Thanksgiving weekend in 1999, seven days before what would have been Mekye Malcolm's eighteenth birthday, Ms. Watkins, Hollis Watkins, Sr., and four of Mekye's brothers and sisters gathered at the Durham cemetery where Mekye is buried amid a sea of flat gravestones. His relatives, arms linked, each took turns remembering, singing, and praying.

"He had a thin skin," said his brother John, "but a thick threshold for pain."

As she has done nearly every month since he died, Ms. Watkins placed a bouquet of fresh lilies and daffodils in the steel vase at the site. As she turned to leave, she mouthed the inscription on the stone over his grave: "Peace, Mekye. We wish you peace."

KERBY CASEY GUERRA, 1985—1999

The day Kerby Casey Guerra killed herself, the thirteen-year-old wore a perfect mask of happiness.

A day earlier, Kerby's mother, Donna Guerra, had treated her to a manicure at a fashionable Colorado Springs, Colorado, salon, and Kerby seemed elated. The eighth-grader was transferring from a school she hated, and things finally were starting to look up. That evening, March 19, 1999, the Guerras took Kerby's sister, Kristy Hignite, out to celebrate her thirtieth birthday and asked Kerby to baby-sit her niece and nephew, something the responsible girl had done dozens of times before.

At 9:30 P.M., Kerby's sister called to check in. Kerby told her that the children were fine and that she planned to watch the movie *Mulan* and go to sleep.

But after tucking five-year-old Elizabeth and seven-year-old Jeremy into their beds upstairs, Kerby ransacked the house to find a key to the cabinet where her sister's husband, an Army officer stationed in South Korea, kept a Winchester rifle and ammunition. She unplugged the phone, turned the radio on full blast, then placed her mouth over the rifle's barrel and fired.

When her parents and sister returned at 1:15 A.M., after going on to a club after dinner, her sister was the first to stumble onto the gruesome scene. "Kerby's face was gone. Her brains were out of her head on the kitchen floor. There was blood everywhere," Ms. Hignite said recently. "I wanted to pick her up and put her back together," Kerby's mother said.

Next to Kerby's body was a blood-soaked suicide note that read, "I'm sorry I lied. I love you." In another room, she'd left presents for her niece and nephew: drawings of animals with wings.

"We always thought Kerby was a big, tough girl," Ms. Hignite said. "Really, she was sad and scared inside."

The Guerras' tidy house, on a quiet street in Colorado Springs, is like an advertisement for an antiques magazine, with cuckoo clocks, hand-carved wooden ornaments, and a needlework picture on the wall that reads "Happy Home." But the dozens of portraits of the brown-haired girl that adorn the house are the most prominent decoration.

A year after her death, Kerby's upstairs bedroom is much as she left it, a porthole into the preoccupations of a girl on the cusp of adolescence. Elaborate porcelain dolls perch on high ledges. On the bookshelves are such classics as *Little Women* and *Jane Eyre*. There's a *Children's Illustrated Bible*, a book on how to ask about sex, and several about angels. Kerby's many pets—she had turtles, frogs, and hamsters—once competed for space here with her impressive teddy bear collection.

Kerby's twenty-seven-year-old sister Stacy Barrington describes her as "proper" compared with most of her peers. "She didn't drink beer or smoke. She'd get disgusted if someone would even say a curse word," Ms. Barrington said. The Guerras kept strict control over Kerby's media intake, monitoring her Web surfing and banning all R-rated films.

After Larry Guerra, a thirty-nine-year-old insurance claims adjuster, married Donna, forty-seven, they moved from another part of Colorado Springs with their family (Ms. Guerra has three children from a previous marriage) to this community because they appreciated its wholesomeness. The headlines in the local newspaper paint a picture of a quiet life, with stories headlined "Clean Sidewalk Reminders" and "Holiday Food Safety Tips."

But the Guerras were drawn here mostly because they had heard the schools were top-notch. The newly constructed Eagleview Middle School, nestled in the salmon-colored foothills of the Rocky Mountains and flanked by affluent homes, is the jewel of School District 20, which encompasses Colorado Springs.

When she started sixth grade, Kerby landed a spot in the band, playing clarinet, and was enjoying composing poems in English class. Soon, though, school became intolerable.

Plump and bespectacled in a school dominated by fashion-conscious students from well-to-do families, Kerby was like a doe in a den of wolves. From the day she arrived, friends and family members say, some popular boys teased Kerby about her weight and taunted her, saying she bought her clothes at K-mart. Those same students, they say, also hurled ethnic, racial, and sexual slurs at Kerby. "They called her 'whore' and 'Mexican white trash,'" said Kerby's mother, who is white. Mr. Guerra's family comes from Mexico. Though Kerby was adopted at birth, her biological parents were also Latino and white.

One of Kerby's classmates, fourteen-year-old Krysten Gregor, who has a white father and an African-American mother, said Kerby often was hassled by other students just for being Krysten's friend. "They called her 'nigger lover,'" said Krysten, "and 'bitch.'"

Dusty McCullough, another of Kerby's friends, said that many times other students held Kerby and kicked her and threw her against lockers. "Since I'm short, they'd make fun of me, too," said the fourteen-year-old boy.

To avoid her oppressors, Kerby's friends say, she would hide in the girls' restroom and avoid classes where she might run into those students. When Ms. Barrington, Kerby's sister, complained to Eagleview's principal, Ross McAskill, about the harassment, he "shrugged it off," she maintains.

"He told me she needed to get a backbone," Ms. Barrington said. Kerby's tormentors were never adequately punished, according to the Guerras.

Kerby began to slash her wrists, but hid the scars so her parents wouldn't see. She binged and purged food. Her grades plummeted from B's to F's.

Then one night in January of 1999, Kerby swallowed a mix of the narcotic Demerol, antibiotics, and Xantac cold medicine—all pinched from her parents' medicine cabinet. She had written a suicide note, in the tentative handwriting of a child, that said, "Dear Mommy and Daddy, I know my death will shock you, but I had to do it. All my life I've been teased and harassed. I just couldn't stand it anymore." Rushed to the hospital, her stomach pumped of the toxins, Kerby was admitted that night to a psychiatric facility and put on the antidepressant Paxil.

While their daughter was in the hospital, the Guerras made plans to transfer her to another school. Ms. Guerra said that when Kerby left the facility, "She felt better. She had a positive outlook."

Less than two months later, on March 18, Kerby herself arranged a meeting with the principal. Though she was leaving the school, she wanted to lobby for a support group for other students who were harassed. The meeting didn't go well, but Kerby hid the depth of her disappointment from her family and friends. The next night, in her final note, she apologized to her parents for lying about feeling okay. Then she shot herself.

In the past, children as young as Kerby very rarely killed themselves. But the United States' suicide rate for the youngest victims is increasing faster than at any time since statisticians began recording the data, even though the overall number is still small.

In 1997, 303 children ages ten to fourteen committed suicide, a 120 percent leap since 1980. Experts point to a number of possible reasons why younger children, some still in elementary school, are now more likely to take their own lives: a larger number of unstable households, an increase in drug use, and a more stressful world for competitive high achievers. Better reporting may also account for a small part of the increase, experts say.

But many psychiatrists suggest that the suicide rate is higher mainly because children are far more likely to be depressed than they used to be.

For many years, the prevailing psychiatric belief was that children and adolescents couldn't experience clinical depression. The profession largely embraced Sigmund Freud's theory that depression was anger turned inward by the superego and that since children's unconscious wasn't fully developed, they couldn't get depressed. The idea was that children weren't self-reflective enough to stew about their troubles.

In the twenty-first century, however, it is generally accepted in psychiatric circles that depression doesn't spare the young.

One in five children under age eighteen suffers a mood disorder, from obsessive-compulsive disorder to depression to bipolar disorder, according to the National Institute for Mental Health. While children as young as four have been diagnosed with depression, it generally appears in those between the ages of twelve and fourteen, according to Johns Hopkins professor Dr. Jamison.

"Puberty brings with it a whirlpool of emotions and a steady increase in the prevalence of major psychiatric disorders," she writes in *Night Falls Fast: Understanding Suicide.*

A 1999 report on mental health released by the U.S. Surgeon General estimates that at least 90 percent of children and adolescents who commit suicide were diagnosed with a mental disorder before their deaths.

Research shows that depression is linked to imbalances in the brain's neurological components and that this faulty chemistry is largely inherited. People who suffer from depression have low levels of a common neurotransmitter called serotonin, a chemical linked to pain perception.

People with depressive illness often lose their will to go to school or work, and their appetite and energy levels decrease for prolonged periods—a condition that is profoundly more devastating than what most people term "the blues."

In his memoir, *Darkness Visible*, author William Styron compares depression to suffocation: "The despair comes to resemble the diabolical discomfort of being imprisoned in a fiercely overheated room. And because there is no escape from this smothering confinement, it is entirely natural that the victim begins to think ceaselessly of oblivion."

When Kerby Guerra was admitted to the Cleo Wallace Center, she, too, was cocooned in her own misery. The medical records describe her demeanor as alternately tearful and "vegetative." After a week of evaluation and counseling, she was diagnosed as having "multiple depressive symptoms," according to center records.

"She had a mood disorder that required ongoing treatment," said Kim Shirtleff, a family therapist in private practice who treated Kerby in the emergency room. She was
given a prescription of 40 milligrams of Paxil, which is
meant to blunt feelings of hopelessness.

But when Kerby walked back into the 1,100-student
Eagleview Middle School at the end of January 1999, she felt
exposed to the elements again. Joanne Gregor, the mother
of Kerby's friend Krysten, described Eagleview's atmosphere
in Darwinian terms. "In this school, it's survival of the
fittest," she contended.

"Kids who get harassed so much go one of two ways,"
said Kerby's friend Dusty McCullough, who was eager to
escape to high school himself. "They want revenge or they
want out."

Across the country, the chaos churning inside students' heads is often unlocked by environmental stress, said
University of Illinois professor Dorothy Espelage, who is an
expert on bullying. Youngsters who are bullied, she said,
are more likely to commit suicide. Kerby's depression and
the environment at school were a fatal combination, Ms.
Shirtleff said, after hearing a description of the situation
from Kerby and her parents. "She wasn't able to cope."

In late 1999, the Guerras filed a formal complaint with
the U.S. Department of Education's office for civil rights,
claiming that the school had failed to protect Kerby from
racial harassment. Racial slurs violated their child's legal
right to a public education in a safe environment, the Guerras argued. Minority students make up about 11 percent of
the school's enrollment.

In their complaint, the Guerras also claim that they were denied critical information that could have saved their daughter's life. A year before Kerby committed suicide, she told a counselor that she was suicidal, and that information, they contend, was never reported to them. "My daughter went to people in the school, she went to counselors and teachers, and no one helped," Ms. Guerra said. "We wanted to come forward and say we won't take this anymore."

Meanwhile, one of Kerby's teachers said she was livid about the way the school, in her view, was being used as a scapegoat for a family's problems. "I think she was disturbed," the teacher said about Kerby in an interview. "You are dealing with a hysterical girl trying to get attention."

And Nanette Anderson, the spokeswoman for the 16,900-student school district, said Eagleview Middle School's environment is far from hostile.

"When I walked down the hall at Eagleview," she said, "I saw middle school behavior, but I didn't see anything violent."

Though she would not comment on Mr. McAskill's specific actions, Ms. Anderson said the school's response to the Guerras' complaints about their daughter's harassment was adequate. "The claims were investigated, and the district found the administration handled the complaints correctly," she said.

She also disputes the Guerras' claim that the counselor didn't inform them of her session with Kerby. "The parents did know about her visit," Ms. Anderson said. Kerby would still be alive, the district spokeswoman added, if she hadn't had access to a gun.

Donna Guerra says she feels physically sick when she thinks about Kerby scavenging for the key to her brother-in-law's gun cabinet.

"We did everything they told us," Ms. Guerra said. "We locked the medicine cabinet. We did just what the doctors said. We just didn't get that stupid gun out of the house."

PART III. UNPREPARED FOR THE WORST

ALL SCHOOLS CONDUCT fire drills, and many have detailed plans for coping with floods, hurricanes, or earthquakes. They employ nurses to vaccinate students against diseases. These days, some even practice for the one-in-a-million chance that an armed intruder will go on a shooting spree.

But most schools are unprepared to deal with a far more common threat to their students: Suicide is the third-leading killer of ten- to nineteen-year-olds in the United States, yet only one in ten schools has a plan to prevent it.

Most schools that teach suicide prevention generally opt for quick units in health class or school assemblies. Typically, they show videos of healthy-looking adolescents who have survived a suicide attempt. But psychologists warn that such an approach can do more harm than good.

Whether owing to a lack of financial resources or to ignorance or denial of the problem, few schools are tackling suicide prevention in a comprehensive way that research suggests can save lives.

And there are lives to be saved. Youth suicide rates have tripled in the past thirty years, reaching an all-time high in the 1990s. On average, one out of every three districts loses a student to suicide each year—sometimes on their own campuses.

In fact, a quarter of the deaths on school grounds are suicides. Students who kill themselves on school property tend to do so in highly public venues—such as their classrooms or the school parking lot. A fourteen-year-old girl hanged herself in the restroom of her New York City middle school in 1999. That same year, the seventeen-year-old captain of the football team in a small Connecticut town doused his body with gasoline and ignited himself on the practice field.

"It usually takes multiple deaths on school grounds to grab administrators' attention," said Scott Poland, the psychological services director for the Cypress Fairbanks, Texas, public schools, who has written a book on suicide prevention. Some districts are paying dearly in court, Mr. Poland added. "Educators need to take this seriously."

Although the damage awards against school districts in student suicide cases are up significantly, some district lawyers caution educators against undue alarm. "School districts shouldn't get the wrong impression that they should run around like chickens with their heads cut off and do suicide prevention when they have limited resources," said Leslie Land, who successfully defended the Springfield, Oregon, school district in a 1999 suicide case.

Many parental-rights advocates, meanwhile, argue that a child's emotional problems are a family matter and that schools are inappropriate venues to broach the issues of life and death.

"Who are these people that they should assert their views on other people's children?" asked Phyllis Schlafly, president of the Eagle Forum, a conservative family advocacy group based in Alton, Illinois. She calls class discussions of suicide "death education."

"School is for academic purposes, not psychological ones," she said.

Few would argue with the idea that an all-out suicide watch tests the principle of *in loco parentis*.

When the courts first held that public schools have special duties as stewards of the nation's young people for eight hours a day, they probably didn't envision principals patrolling their buildings to stop Jane from jumping off the roof.

But, then, there wasn't as much roof jumping back then.

The Latin term *in loco parentis*—literally, "in the place of parents"—was first used by the Romans to refer to the Greek slaves whom they employed to tutor their children. So that the Roman children would respect their low-ranked teachers, the Roman masters delegated their parental power temporarily so the Greeks could discipline the pupils in their care.

The U.S. courts, having inherited the doctrine from English law, also applied the concept to help teachers keep students in their seats. Over the years, various courts conferred broad supervisory power on schools to control unruly students, using the doctrine at times to sanction paddling and other corporal punishment.

Along with the power to discipline students came certain responsibilities to protect students from harm. In recent years, the courts have taken this guardianship status further

by holding schools liable for negligence if they fail to protect a child who is harassed or sexually abused by another
student at school. In the past twenty years, several courts
extended the surrogate parental obligation further still, finding that schools have a legal obligation to take "reasonable
steps" to protect students from hurting themselves.

Whether a student commits suicide in the bedroom or
in the school's locker room, the courts are sending a message
to schools that they can no longer stand on the sidelines, said
Mr. Lieberman, school psychologist with the Los Angeles
public schools, who has testified on behalf of school districts.

The number of lawsuits filed against school districts
claiming negligence in student suicides has increased tenfold
in the past twenty years, Mr. Lieberman estimates. For
every suicide case that goes to trial, at least twenty are settled out of court, he said. The national publicity over the
flood of school shootings in the late 1990s has helped
prompt a shower of legal claims against schools.

"Parents are now aware they can sue. Every one of the
lawsuits from West Paducah, Kentucky, to Springfield, Oregon, has brought a national awareness that one can litigate
against schools for their failure to provide a safe environment for children," Mr. Lieberman said.

Many school employees are now buying liability insurance in case district plans don't protect them. These plans
are separate from the school district's plan, which often
protects only the district. "It's sleep insurance," said Doug
Kocher, a director of property and casualty at Forrest T.
Jones Inc., a Kansas City, Missouri, insurance broker that
covers more than 150,000 teachers. "They want to have
something to fall back on."

Although federal law requires schools to report to authorities if they suspect that a student is being abused by his or her parents, no state requires schools to notify parents if a student expresses suicidal thoughts.

When schools are found to be liable in a child's suicide, legal experts say, it's generally for negligence: They could have "foreseen the suicidal risk" of the student, or they knew of the student's intent to harm himself or herself and failed to take "responsible" steps to prevent it. Some notable cases point out how schools have failed to step up to the plate:

• In a watershed case in 1995, a federal district court in Tampa, Florida, found the Polk County school board guilty of negligence in thirteen-year-old Shawn Wyke's death and awarded his mother $167,000. The day before Shawn's suicide in 1989, another student told the assistant principal that he had discovered Shawn trying to hang himself in the school restroom. But the administrator failed to notify the boy's mother about the incident. The next day, the fifth grader hanged himself from an oak tree in his backyard.

• In January 1997, a student at a Longview, Washington, high school told her mother that her ex-boyfriend was talking about killing himself and that he was standing in front of a mirror every night with a gun to his head. That day, the girlfriend's mother told the school counselor about Nick Shoff's comments. But instead of notifying the boy's parents himself, which was the school's policy, or summoning the fifteen-year-old out of class for a psychological evaluation, the counselor asked the girlfriend's mother to call the Shoffs. She didn't call in time. That night, Nick went home and fatally shot himself.

The school district settled out of court with his parents for $690,000.

• A 1991 case against the Montgomery County, Maryland, board of education stemmed from junior high school student telling a counselor that their friend was making suicidal statements. When a counselor questioned Nicole Eisel about those comments, the thirteen-year-old denied that she was going to hurt herself, and the counselor chose not to notify her parents. A week later, the girl was killed in a murder-suicide pact. A state appeals court found the counselors negligent in their duty to warn the parents, arguing that the counselors should have been able to "foresee" the suicide despite the girl's denials.

Whether such legal claims are well-founded or not, these lawsuits often are driven by parents' desire, or need, to assign blame, some experts say.

"Who else are you going to sue? You aren't going to sue yourself for not helping your child. You aren't going to sue your psychiatrist," said Julie Underwood, the general counsel for the National School Boards Association (NSBA). "Schools can't be protectors of all children."

"A lot of this is misdirected grief," psychologist Lieberman added. "Parents say Satan did it. Marilyn Manson did it. We simplify it and put it up on the shelf so we can understand it. People have to put that anger somewhere."

It's no simple task to detect a child's suicidal intent. Metal detectors and surveillance cameras may nab gun-toting teenagers, but they don't pick up inner turmoil.

Most U.S. schools—58 percent—discuss suicide prevention in some academic course during the school year, according to a 1995 survey of school health programs published in the *Journal of School Health*. Those units, which typically last three hours or less, usually include video docudramas of teenagers who survived a suicide attempt, use shocking statistics designed to get students' attention, and provide information on where teenagers should go for help.

Publications now on the market range from mail-order suicide prevention kits at $6.65 apiece, which are essentially lists of warning signs, to higher-priced textbooks used in health classes. Many schools hire lecturers to speak to large assemblies on the subject. Like the ubiquitous drug awareness programs, in which police officers try to "scare kids straight" with the gritty realities of addiction, many suicide prevention programs now employ medical experts to deliver a similar jolt of shock therapy.

In his presentations to high school students, Dr. Victor Victoroff, the chairman emeritus of psychiatry at Huron Road Medical Center in Cleveland, Ohio, shows slides of teenagers who attempt suicide and end up in emergency rooms: a girl who had her stomach pumped, a boy with his face blown off by a gunshot blast, a girl with her wrists carved up. "I'll use any means to cut through the romantic haze. I want them to know suicide is a painful experience," Dr. Victoroff said.

The general view among mental health professionals is that talking about suicide can help prevent teenagers from committing it. But there is no evidence that short lectures in classrooms or noisy, packed school assemblies, or even visits to the morgue, have any measurable effect on preventing teenagers from killing themselves. And some of the approaches may actually aggravate the situation for the most vulnerable students.

In one of the most rigorous evaluations of suicide prevention programs, Dr. David Shaffer, a professor of psychiatry at Columbia University, found that the most commonly
used suicide awareness programs in schools often did more
harm than good.

In his 1987 study, Dr. Shaffer evaluated several widely
used programs with 1,000 students in six New Jersey high
schools. While there was no evidence that the didactic classroom discussions caused emotional distress among students
as a whole, neither did they alter the disturbing attitudes of
those students who said that "in certain situations, suicide
was a reasonable solution to one's problems."

Moreover, the study found, those students who were
already contemplating suicide were more distressed after
being exposed to the lessons. "Talking about it might stim-
ulate what has been bottled up, and that's not necessarily a
good thing," said Dr. Shaffer.

Such findings have emboldened critics who believe suicide prevention courses ought to be dropped. "These death
and dying courses can have dangerous consequences," said
Ms. Schlafly of the Eagle Forum. "Some children may be
tripped over the edge."

But schools may be able to drive down the youth suicide rate if they employ very specific methods.

Preliminary findings from a study by University of
Washington researchers suggest that students who practice
solving difficult dilemmas in their lives though role-playing
in group sessions with other students twice a week are less
likely to be depressed or to exhibit suicidal behavior than
those who do not take part in such programs.

The American Association of Suicidology, a nonprofit
organization based in Washington, D.C., dedicated to

understanding and preventing suicide, suggests that one way to curb suicides is to train school personnel—from bus drivers to custodians to teachers—to recognize certain behavioral clues that a student is at risk: A sustained case of the blues, discarding valuable possessions, emotional volatility, and suicidal statements all hint at trouble.

Teachers might also read student essays for more than their literary value. A 1986 study of students' work in several schools found 500 poems that contained suicidal references but that were returned to students without comment or follow-up.

One of the students, an eleven-year-old boy, turned in an essay titled "Suicide Mistake" in which he outlined his own death in detail. That night, he killed himself just as he'd described.

Teachers are often reluctant to talk to their colleagues about students for fear that they will violate a student's privacy rights, said the NSBA's Ms. Underwood. "Students' privacy gets so drilled into their heads, and unfortunately they sometimes get snagged by it."

If teachers detect morbid preoccupations, however, they should be discreet about revealing them, Mr. Poland said. In his book, he cites the case of a Denver teacher who intercepted a note written by a seventh grader and read the personal details about his melancholy state to the class. The twelve-year-old boy committed suicide later that day.

Another way to put a dent in the youth suicide rate is to persuade teenagers to tell adults when they know other students have such intentions, even though it might be viewed as tattling.

The unwritten code of silence among students has to be broken, said Mr. Flatt, who, through the Nashville-based

Jason Foundation, named for his dead son, trains teenagers to take their friends' morbid musings seriously. "In 70 percent of all teen suicides, another teen knew about it and did nothing," he said.

Though no formal research has been done, Mr. Flatt is encouraged by the results so far: Since he launched the Teens Helping Teens program in 1997, he has received forty-two letters from young people who said their friends' "snitching" had saved their lives.

Many experts say the subject is particularly difficult to teach—even more sensitive than AIDS, sex, or drugs—because talking about suicide has long been considered taboo.

The ancient Greeks and Romans condemned suicide as an offense against the state because it deprived society of a productive member. Many religious denominations have held that suicide victims are condemned to hell and have barred their burial in sacred ground and shrouded their memory in shame.

A more compassionate view of suicide victims has emerged in recent years. For example, the Reverend Arnaldo Pangrazzi, a Roman Catholic priest in Italy, expressed the current official Catholic teaching in a 1984 newsletter article: "Churches should teach compassion toward those who take their own lives and judgment should be left to God." The idea is not to promote self-murder as an acceptable avenue to solve problems, but rather to avoid helping it along by making people suffer in silence.

Still, at a suicide prevention conference in Nashville in 1999, Surgeon General Satcher said despite the progress made in churches and religious institutions, the overarching taboo remains. In a year in which 30,000 Americans would commit suicide, Dr. Satcher argued that the country must view suicide as a public-health epidemic. The country should rally its resources to fight this problem just as the Red Cross keeps blankets and food on hand to rescue people from famine, flood, or other natural disasters.

"It's time for us to move from shame and stigma to support," said Dr. Satcher. Because a majority of teenagers who kill themselves suffer some type of diagnosable mental health problem, the best way schools can ward off more suicides is to usher troubled children to the nearest mental health professional, Dr. Satcher said. The dip in the teenage suicide rate in the late 1990s is partly attributable to better screening of children for mental health problems, some experts say.

One of the most promising places in this country to thwart a suicide may be the school nurse's office.

In a ten-month University of Washington study of fourteen Seattle schools, students who were deemed at risk for dropping out were interviewed in two-hour sessions by a nurse or social worker, who asked them a series of questions about their mood and called their parents or a hospital if they expressed suicidal inclinations.

Those who participated in the psychological interview program were 54 percent less likely to have suicidal thoughts or act on them in the months following the session than those who did not participate, the study found.

The potential for preventing teenage suicide through screenings such as these is huge, simply because of the volume of visitors to a school nurse's office.

Of all the children in the United States who seek mental health services, half get them at school. But states spend less than 1 percent of their education budgets on mental health services in schools. With limited funds to hire psychologists and social workers, most schools don't have staff members who are trained to diagnose mental health conditions.

"You have to know the difference between a joking teen and one who has a knife under their bed or has already counted out the pills," said Leslie Kraft, who runs Columbia University's well-regarded Teen Screen program, in which social workers and nurses are trained to identify teenagers in four New York City high schools who are at risk for suicide. About a quarter of the more than 800 students identified in 1999 as being at risk were referred for further evaluation. "We've kept a lot of these kids alive," Ms. Kraft said.

School psychologists like Mr. Lieberman say that one challenge in their job is to make sure students feel comfortable divulging their secrets. All sessions are kept private, as therapy won't be effective otherwise. But a counselor who suspects a child is suicidal has a legal obligation to report it. Typically, the counselor will talk with a student and ask permission to get help for the student. For example, if a boy attempts or confesses that he plans to hang himself from the jungle gym at recess, then the counselor will call the boy's parents and perhaps have him admitted to a psychiatric ward until he is out of danger.

Experts say that in the best of all possible worlds, children's emotional deficits would be catalogued in kindergarten. Spotlighting and giving early treatment to children with short attention spans, school phobias, or short fuses could greatly reduce problems in later grades, they say.

Minimizing exposure to media reports of the tragedy can also reduce the chances of "copycat" suicides, some experts believe. In the weeks after the highly publicized Columbine High School shootings in Colorado, suicide attempts peaked in several districts nationwide.

Schools can play a role in reducing youth suicide simply by making their schools as welcoming as possible. Most school employees may labor to provide happy environments for students, but some observers warn that many schools are places where bullying is rampant, cliques are ruthless, and teachers are too harried to care.

In a 1999 survey of 558 sixth, seventh, and eighth graders at a suburban Illinois middle school, researchers from the University of Illinois at Urbana-Champaign found that 80 percent of the students reported that they had bullied another classmate in the past thirty days. Most of the self-acknowledged bullies said they were also harassed themselves. Children who are repeatedly harassed are more likely to kill themselves, some separate studies have found.

The national push to raise academic standards and hold schools more accountable for their students' performance has also placed new pressures on children, some health educators say. Performing well on new, high-stakes tests can be just as stressful for some students as a verbal assault by the class bully.

"They don't give awards to the mediocre," said one school counselor.

Gifted students who are competing for slots at top colleges can just as easily be overwhelmed by pressures for them to succeed, said Mr. Lieberman, who points to a Los Angeles high school senior with a 4.0 grade point average who killed himself in 1999 after he was rejected by UCLA.

In a survey of teenagers on the reasons why they attempted suicide, school pressures ranked in the top three, along with a romantic split and family problems. "You can't separate out students' emotional report card from their academic report card," said Harvard's Dr. Pollack.

He and others suggest a fairly straightforward solution to improving students' mental health: expressing affection. Studies dating to the 1960s have shown that animals that are deprived of physical affection when they are young tend to exhibit more aggressive and violent behavior later in life.

Tiffany Field, a University of Miami researcher who runs the Touch Institute, applied that theory to the classroom in her study of interactions between teachers and students in France and the United States. Ms. Field found that the French students, whose teachers were more physical with them (whether to show discipline or affection), were better behaved and less aggressive than American students, who had less physical contact with their teachers.

Ms. Field laments reports that many U.S. teachers are reluctant to hug students for fear that their gestures will be misinterpreted as sexual. "We are less touchy-feely because there are more lawyers around," she said, "even though setting limits with affection is the best way to be a teacher or a parent."

Of course, suicide prevention experts acknowledge, many measures that might reduce the youth suicide rate are out of educators' hands.

Researchers often cite a British study to show that reducing access to deadly means can greatly drive down the suicide rate. In 1957, the carbon monoxide content of domestic cooking gas in Britain was 12 percent, and self-asphyxiation accounted for 40 percent of all suicides there.

By 1971, a year after the introduction of natural gas reduced the carbon monoxide levels to 2 percent, asphyxiation accounted for less than 10 percent of suicides, and the overall suicide rate in Britain plummeted by 26 percent.

In the United States, two-thirds of people under eighteen who commit suicide use a firearm. Dr. Shires, with the Suicide Prevention Research Center, advocates minimizing access to handguns. But he expresses doubt that such measures would make a serious dent in suicide rates. "If they don't do it with guns, they will do it with something else," he said.

What perturbs Dr. Shires most is what he sees as the medical profession's poor record at diagnosing and treating young patients' psychological pain.

Dr. Shires' research found that 70 percent of all people who attempt suicide have seen their family physician within thirty days before they make the attempt. But many medical doctors are not well versed in distinguishing between serious emotional distress and fleeting adolescent angst.

Dr. Shires prescribes a multipronged approach to fighting suicide: If physicians were better trained, more students had caring adults in their lives from infancy on, and schools were better prepared to identify troubled children and get them the help they needed quickly, the youth suicide rate would surely plummet, he says.

In light of the societal forces driving children to suicide, counselor Linda Taylor says, schools that take up the challenge have to be warned that they can't save every child.

Ms. Taylor, a counselor at the Los Angeles public schools' well-respected mental health clinic, tells the story of a rambunctious ten-year-old girl she was treating years ago for attention deficit hyperactivity disorder. One evening, the child's mother told the fifth grader to clean up her room and not to come out until it was clean. The girl hanged herself from a belt in her bedroom closet.

"Everyone was devastated," said Ms. Taylor, who added that though the girl's father had recently died, the family was close, and there was no clear sign the child had serious emotional problems. "We felt, my God, what did we miss? How did we not see what was coming?"

ALONE ON THE RANGE

An hour before pale yellow light begins to lap across the fields of winter wheat, Tim Harmon is already whizzing down the highway that cuts through the South Dakota hinterland to reach his first patient before the school bell rings. Like a one-man emotional emergency room, the tireless school psychologist bolts into a classroom and conducts a fifteen-minute one-on-one counseling session with a student who threatened to hang himself last year. Then, satisfied that the boy is stabilized, he speeds off to his next case, at a school more than 100 miles east.

Mr. Harmon treks 3,000 miles a month, spreading his time among five school systems flung across the vast Dakota plains, conducting IQ tests, unearthing tales of child abuse, and sometimes thwarting a suicide.

In 1999, he saved a sixteen-year-old girl poised to leap out of a school's third-floor restroom window. "I just happened to be there in time to grab her and pull her back in," he said.

Half the schoolchildren in the United States who seek mental health care get it at school. But districts, with rare exceptions, give low priority to professional mental health services. As a result, school psychologists and social workers are spread thin. In the United States, the ratio of school psychologists to students is about 1 to 1,500.

With a bigger-than-average caseload—nearly 2,000 students—in one of the most sparsely populated regions of the country, Mr. Harmon is spread thinner than most.

He is quick to point out that South Dakota has more garden-variety psychoses per capita than most regions of the country. The state ranks third in the nation for teenage suicides, with a rate that is double the national average: Roughly eleven of every 100,000 ten- to nineteen-year-olds in the state take their own lives.

At the same time, the economically struggling state devotes little money to mental health care. Fiscally conservative lawmakers recently abandoned the state's requirement that every school district hire a guidance counselor—people mental health experts see as well-placed antennae to detect and transmit valuable information about students in trouble.

Under such circumstances, the eighty school psychologists in South Dakota—like their overworked colleagues in other states—are asked to do little more than conduct the mandatory diagnostic tests for special education and gifted classes. But thirty-three-year-old Mr. Harmon deplores desk duty. He sees his job as psychological triage: "You leave the little fires burning until you can put out the big ones."

Racing across the monotonously flat landscape—interrupted only by haystacks, grain elevators, and the occasional lonesome clump of trees—Mr. Harmon said one reason teenagers here tend to be more despondent than most is that they and their families see few opportunities on the horizon.

As he listens to President Clinton over the car radio issuing an upbeat assessment of the nation's robust economy at the start of the new millennium, Mr. Harmon shakes his head: "The economy isn't booming over here."

In the late 1980s, 90 percent of the families in this southern swath of South Dakota farmed. A decade later, 60 percent did. Farm prices have sunk to historic lows; people are selling their equipment and taking jobs at truck stops or migrating to Sioux Falls or Rapid City.

As he pulls his weather-beaten Chevrolet Prizm into the Platte High School parking lot, Mr. Harmon points out that the frustrations of out-of-work farmers can translate into domestic violence.

On a school assignment to compile a wish list for 2000, one fourth grader Mr. Harmon counsels expressed a typical sentiment: "I wish crop prices would go up so Mom and Dad would stop fighting."

As he enters the teachers' lounge at Platte, Mr. Harmon finds out about three cases of child abuse, one divorce, and a parent's suicide attempt in less time than it takes teachers to finish their morning coffee and muffins.

Then comes the most bizarre tale of the morning: A junior told her teacher that her parents have been holding parties at their home where they offered up her and her two sisters as sex slaves to their drug-addicted guests. "The kids were offered as door prizes," Mr. Harmon said.

Before leaving the school, Mr. Harmon heads upstairs to visit one of his regular clients—Jeff Vanderheiden, a hulking, six-foot-three-inch junior who suffers from severe depression. The eighteen-year-old threatened to kill himself twice before anyone called Mr. Harmon for help last year. As soon as Mr. Harmon found out about Jeff's second suicide attempt, he drove the teenager to the nearest hospital himself—120 miles away. Jeff needs regular psychological counseling, but the nearest clinic is ninety miles from school. County mental health clinics already are bulging with adult patients, and they don't make house calls. If Mr. Harmon didn't drive more than two hours from his home to counsel the adolescent at school every other week, no one would.

And Jeff says he's grateful to have someone to talk to.

"This year, I literally wanted to end it all. I had a difficult time making friends," he said after a brief chat with Mr. Harmon. "Tim helps me. He's like concrete. My road was so bumpy until he filled it out with his advice."

One school on Mr. Harmon's regular rounds, Kimball High School, is so small that the principal also serves as a counselor—a role Mr. Harmon said is counterproductive. Students are reluctant to reach out to their chief disciplinarian if they have an emotional problem.

Since he can't provide one-on-one therapy sessions with every student in his 145-square-mile region, Mr. Harmon often uses the academic testing sessions he's required to conduct to determine whether a youngster is having emotional difficulties.

In a given month, he administers thirty tests; while he's diagnosing verbal acuity and reasoning skills, he's also on the lookout for signs of depression or sociopathic tendencies, any sign that the child is off-kilter.

One of his patients on one cold winter day in 1999 was a chatty six-year-old boy who sat in an overheated school room, zipping through a routine IQ test. As the boy flipped through dozens of cue cards of animal pictures and parallelograms designed to test memory, Mr. Harmon casually asked the kindergartner about his family. His father, he said, had moved out of the house, and he hadn't seen him much since.

Mr. Harmon tracked down the boy's teacher after the test to tell her about the family situation. The teacher said the father's absence might explain why the youngster had been more withdrawn lately. It might also explain why the bright boy scored below average on the IQ test.

"He may be having emotional problems due to the family's instability," said Mr. Harmon, who said he would retest the boy at a later date.

After the session, Mr. Harmon drove the 100 miles back to his hometown school in Kimball for a session of play therapy with a volatile fifth grader.

In a cramped utility room stuffed with broomsticks and cleaning supplies—the only quiet spot available at Kimball Elementary School—Mr. Harmon asked the boy to set up the rules for a made-up game called Pinball 2000. Mr. Harmon said the ten-year-old has "anger control" issues—he once threw his three-year-old sister down a flight of stairs—and he needs to learn how to obey rules because his home environment is unstructured.

"Parents aren't raising kids with rules," Mr. Harmon said. "They should discipline them while they're young, and later give children freedom. But they do the opposite: give the young ones freedom and then micromanage the teens, which just makes kids aggressive."

Many of the parents here really don't want his help. In fact, the prevailing sentiment in the rural communities he serves is that the church, not psychologists, should tend to children's emotional needs. The idea is that psychology goes against the Bible's teachings because it preaches reliance on oneself instead of God.

"They think that psychologists are the spawn of Satan," said Mr. Harmon, who usually introduces himself to parents simply as a school employee to avoid any confrontations.

In addition, the pioneering spirit of self-reliance here has had the effect of muting calls for additional state aid for such services.

Bob Mercer, a spokesman for Governor William J. Janklow, said rural districts in Mr. Harmon's region that are losing population should cut other administrative jobs if they want to hire more counselors. "How do you deliver services in a state where population is declining? They must be more efficient," Mr. Mercer said.

One principal said that with what schools can afford to pay counselors—$27,000 a year—it's hard to find qualified applicants in any case.

Donna Knipers, a special education teacher at Platte High School who functions as a de facto counselor, said she is worried that more students like Jeff are roaming the halls with suicidal thoughts.

"I can trust my gut instincts, but we need someone here who can intervene when there's a crisis," Ms. Knipers said. "I don't feel comfortable handling matters that are literally life and death."

MONEY WOES

The high school needs a new roof. The teachers want a raise. Half the bus fleet needs a maintenance overhaul. Joey is depressed.

Which of these problems is a district most likely to tackle last? When most school boards debate their budget priorities, identifying children with mental health problems doesn't generally rank high on the agenda. But the hidden costs of student woes hover like ghosts in the room.

Nearly 5 million students a year seek refuge from their emotional problems in the company of teachers, coaches, and school counselors. A Connecticut study conducted in the late 1990s found that the number one reason students visited the school health clinic was for mental health or substance abuse problems, not bloody noses or birth control. Most schools already are providing mental health services, experts say; they just aren't getting fully paid for it.

A combination of factors—state and federal funding hasn't kept pace with students' escalating emotional needs, districts fail to lobby for such support, and the public is suspicious of school psychological programs in general—has resulted in a scenario in which resources are stretched thin and students badly in need of help are often given cursory care.

Several studies have shown that screening teenagers for depression and other mental illnesses at school can help reduce the suicide rate. A majority of young people who commit suicide have histories of mental health disorders.

In addition, the National Institute of Mental Health estimates that 9 percent of the nation's students suffer from emotional or behavioral problems that pose a serious barrier to learning.

"This is a forest fire, and we are using buckets," said Mr. Dwyer of the NASP. Few districts calculate how much time their regular staff members devote to counseling students, making referrals, and processing related paperwork, and many don't keep track of exactly how much they spend on professionals to help students cope with extracurricular angst.

But Alan Odden, a professor of education at the University of Wisconsin-Madison, estimates that districts spend roughly 5 percent of their total budgets on "student support services," which include social workers and counselors as well as safety personnel.

Gordon Wrobel, the health care coordinator for the National Association of School Psychologists (NASP), estimates that districts' mental health costs balloon into the millions when one adds in the time that all staff members spend with troubled children on a daily basis. When schools have no personnel designated to provide mental health services, everyone—teachers, principals, and coaches—takes a swing at the problem, he said.

"Education's contribution to [addressing] the national epidemic [of teenage suicide] would stagger even the most liberal politicians," Mr. Wrobel said.

But because more school employees than private physicians or psychologists serve as de facto therapists to the nation's adolescents, their ranks are woefully inadequate to meet the demand, Mr. Wrobel said. A NASP survey found that the average school psychologist has a caseload of 1,500 students; NASP's recommended caseload is 1,000.

School psychologists earn an average of about $49,000 a year, a low salary compared with what their private-sector counterparts can make. That makes it hard to attract and retain qualified professionals.

Yet a lack of trained personnel can, in itself, prove costly. Several districts in the 1980s and 1990s have been hit with negligence lawsuits for failing to refer students who had expressed suicidal intentions for professional help.

Though no one tracks exactly how much states and the federal government spend on school-based health care, experts estimate that it's less than a fraction of 1 percent of their revenue. Spending varies widely from state to state; such expenditures are often governed by how wealthy a state is and how disposed its residents are to paying for such programs. As a result, some states opt to pay for psychiatrists to work in state-of-the-art mental health clinics in schools, while others balk at hiring guidance counselors.

While many factors can influence how many teenagers in a given state commit suicide, one long-term study found that public investments in social services can reduce the suicide toll in general.

A University of Minnesota study published in 1990 compared states' suicide rates with their spending on Medicaid and other public welfare programs over a thirty-year period, with factors such as divorce rates, population density, race, and gender all being equal. Shirley L. Simmerman, a professor of social science at the university and the lead author of the study, found that suicide rates were higher in states that spent less on public welfare programs compared with those that spent more "to meet the needs of people."

For instance, South Dakota, which in 1997 spent $54 per capita on mental health services overall—well below the national average—had the third-highest teenage suicide rate in the nation. By comparison, Connecticut, which spent $99 per capita that year on mental health services, ranked 46th in adolescent suicides. Some officials, meanwhile, argue that the federal government hasn't contributed its share to help schools reduce suicides.

From 1969 to 1994, federal spending on all mental health services rose just 5 percent after adjusting for inflation, according to a report by the federal Substance Abuse and Mental Health Services Administration (SAMHSA).

During the same period, the rates for depression and suicide among youths tripled.

"There's been money spent, but not a lot," said Michael J. English, the director of the division of SAMHSA that oversees youth programs. "No one would suggest we have been close to meeting the needs of children with mental health disorders."

Even when the federal government does promise money, it doesn't always come through, Mr. Wrobel said.

Though the federal government in 1975 required schools to conduct psychological evaluations of students who seek special education services, which includes children with mental illnesses, the government has paid only a portion of the tab. Congress intended the federal government to pick up as much as 40 percent of schools' costs, but the federal contribution has never exceeded 12 percent, Mr. Wrobel said.

One result of the financial strain on school budgets is complaints from parents about shoddy service. In a report titled "A School System in Denial," the National Alliance for the Mentally Ill contends that students with serious emotional problems aren't getting the help they are entitled to by federal law.

The advocacy group, based in Arlington, Virginia, surveyed parents of such students about their schools' services and found that 46 percent of them believed that their children's schools "resisted identifying children with mental illness." And 60 percent said that the schools' individualized educational plans—required for students with disabilities—failed to meet their children's psychological and medical needs. For these parents, it is like taking a feverish child to the doctor and going home with a pat on the back and a lollipop, but no medicine. The schools don't treat them seriously, they say.

A complicated bureaucracy also frequently comes between schools and their money. Districts can apply for mental health care revenue for suicide prevention from a dizzying array of sources: the federal Medicaid program, the federal Maternal Child Health Block Grant, the state education department or health department, the state legislature, private foundations, and local governments.

Mr. Wrobel calls that the "bake sale" model for funding, in which schools get little bits of money here and there and attempt to put together a service. "The patchwork of funding sources has created a labyrinth that befuddles even the most sophisticated financial analysis," he said.

Another obstacle to financing school mental health services is that Medicaid reimbursements for school clinic care create snarls of paperwork. That means only the districts that can spare the personnel to do the administrative tasks can benefit from the program.

Julia Lear, who runs Making the Grade, a Washington, D.C.-based program that provides support to the country's more than 1,000 school-based health clinics, contended that the federal government has purposely made the system of reimbursement for health services so complicated to discourage billing that would drive up Medicaid costs. "They've made it hard for schools, and it wasn't an accident," she asserted.

For their part, federal experts say that schools have taken advantage of the Medicaid program and billed for services that weren't health related.

States such as Montana, which have tried managed care systems to help contain medical costs, also have made providing mental health care for students harder, said Doug Cockran-Roberts, a psychologist at Corvallis Primary School in Corvallis, Montana. "The managed care company put a lid on money spent, and the quality suffered," he said.

But districts sometimes erect their own barriers to getting the financing they seek, said Kathy Christie, a policy analyst for the Education Commission of the States in Denver. With many items on their wish lists, education groups from the teachers' unions to the superintendents' associations seldom lobby for mental health care the way they do for building repairs, metal detectors, or higher teacher salaries, she said.

And because constituents in many states are dubious about using tax dollars to subsidize school mental health counselors, schools need to explain to legislators why they should care, Ms. Christie added.

SAMHSA's Mr. English advised that if educators want more money for such services, they need to tuck mental health care funds into their traditional package of requests when they lobby the federal government for assistance. "Kids are not going to stand up and say, 'I have a mental problem. Come help me,'" Mr. English said.

One effective lobbying tactic that has won revenue to combat smoking, teenage pregnancy, and AIDS is the argument that cash up front saves more money down the road. Mental health screenings, in particular, can be cost savers. Students whose depression is detected and who are then referred for treatment are 50 percent less likely to attempt suicide, a University of Washington study has found. Experts estimate the average cost of an emergency room visit for a suicide attempt to be about $33,000.

Alex Berman, the executive director of the American Association of Suicidology, estimates that each teenager who commits suicide costs society about $500,000 in terms of lost wages and productivity for an average life span.

Dr. Satcher has tried during his tenure as surgeon general to drill this calculus into congressional leaders. In late 1999, Dr. Satcher and Tipper Gore unveiled the nation's first comprehensive suicide prevention strategy. It calls on Congress to enact legislation that would put money into research on the most effective suicide prevention techniques, help reduce the stigma associated with suicide, and foster the availability of state-of-the-art mental health care.

"The federal government isn't spending enough to help kids," said Sen. Harry Reid (D-Nev.), who backed a Senate bill to boost suicide prevention programs. "We spend a lot of money advertising the dangers of AIDS and tobacco, but we need to educate young people on the dangers of suicide."

Mr. English predicted that such an initiative could encounter resistance on Capitol Hill. "But if we can bring people to the bottom line—how do we save our children— then people may start thinking about what this is really about," he said.

SUICIDE MAN

For a school employee, Richard Lieberman has an unusual job description: Keep children from killing themselves.

"They call me Suicide Man," said the upbeat director of the Suicide Prevention Unit for the Los Angeles Unified School District.

Nothing in his school psychology courses in college quite prepared Mr. Lieberman for the task of buoying the spirits of children in a district with a student population of 700,000, the size of a medium-sized metropolis. But, with the help of a district-run mental health clinic, a city teeming with psychological clinics, and a $14 million annual investment from the district's budget for mental health services, the number of student suicides in the district dropped from thirty-five in 1989 to nineteen in 1997.

California lawmakers who provided the seed money for the suicide prevention unit in 1987 credit the Los Angeles school system with helping the state's overall teenage suicide rate shrink while the national rate ballooned. Florida's Miami-Dade County system, with 350,000 students, is believed to be the only other district in the country that has someone on staff whose job specifically is to drive down the teen suicide rate. In explaining his district's success, Mr. Lieberman points to the requirement that every Los Angeles school have a counselor and a crisis team on campus. And those people are trained to handle emotional crises as nimbly as they would emergencies such as earthquakes and mudslides. All schools also have Mr. Lieberman's cell phone number and are told not to hesitate to call if they are in over their heads.

As he inches through the Los Angeles traffic, Mr. Lieberman's beeper and wireless phone buzz and chime in unison. In any given month, Mr. Lieberman and a school counselor—the unit's two-person professional staff—field hundreds of calls from district crisis teams, made up of principals, teachers, and counselors at each of the system's 700 schools.

On a busy morning in the fall of 1999, the calls cover
a smorgasbord of sorrows: A child shows a morbid drawing
to a teacher, another student slashes her arms, while a third
talks about hearing voices "that are making her do things."

When it comes to suicide prevention, Mr. Lieberman
keeps several basic principles in mind:

• School staff members should reject the idea that talking
about suicide with students will increase the likelihood that
they will act on such impulses. Studies have shown that students are less likely to harm themselves if an adult dispels
assumptions about a particular predicament the child
believes to be dire and irreversible.

• Teachers should be alert to warning signs that a student
might be depressed—sudden changes in attitude or sleeping
habits, or drops in grades or attendance.

• Counselors who are trained to keep therapy sessions con-
fidential need to remember the importance of reporting a
student's suicidal intentions. And because students sometimes confess their suicidal feelings in class journals, teachers should take home emergency numbers in case they see a
mention of suicidal intentions in homework.

Mr. Lieberman said he is fortunate to have county-
sponsored backup agencies to aid him in his suicide prevention mission. The Los Angeles County crisis hot line is
open to students twenty-four hours a day. In the cheery
pink office on the city's fashionable west side, five volunteers
speak with the callers in hushed voices.

The reasons for the upbeat decor are obvious. "We
have a lot of hangings, overdoses, kids saying they are going

to drive off cliffs," said Barbara Hornichter, the coordinator for the hot line, which gets more than 100 calls from suicidal young people each month.

Many teenagers who call say they are worried about a friend but are reluctant to get them help. "I say to them: 'You'd rather have an angry friend than a dead friend, right?' " Ms. Hornichter said.

Schools play a crucial part in reducing the risk of copycat suicides. Six students in Los Angeles schools killed themselves within six weeks of the shootings at Columbine High School in Colorado. The suicide prevention unit received ninety-six calls about suicidal teenagers from eighty schools in the two weeks after the April 20, 1999, incident.

After a suicide, especially a widely publicized one, school staff members should be especially attentive to students they suspect might be emboldened to follow suit, Mr. Lieberman said.

Gloria Grenados, a psychiatric social worker at one of the district's most crime-battered schools, is constantly on alert. "We get two suicide attempts a month. I've even had three in a day," said Ms. Grenados, who is a counselor, confessor, and surrogate mother to many of the 4,900 students at Bell High School.

The district strategically deploys professional social workers such as Ms. Grenados, in addition to the crisis teams, in 200 of the system's neediest schools. Bell High, which sits in a poor South Central Los Angeles neighborhood, used to be notorious for suicides, averaging two a year in the early 1990s. Since Ms. Grenados arrived in 1993, not one Bell student has committed suicide, despite a flood of threats.

One day in the fall of 1999, Ms. Grenados clicked on the laptop computer in her office to display her current caseload. With each fresh screen, a collection of student woes appeared: a fifteen-year-old boy on antipsychotic drugs who attempted suicide at school by tying a cord from his sweatpants around his neck; a fourteen-year-old girl who has a two-year-old child she detests and neglects; a teenage girl whose mother died of brain cancer, and who then contracted a sexually transmitted disease from her father, who had raped her. "This is heavy-duty stuff," Ms. Grenados said. "So many of these kids have lost parents to death, substance abuse. . . . They are so glad that someone is willing to listen to the pain they have harbored for so long."

Ms. Grenados requires that her "hard cases"—students who have expressed suicidal thoughts—check in to her office daily. If they cut class, or are even an hour late, she calls parents or the police. If parents fail to take a clearly suicidal teenager to get psychiatric care, the district often reports them to the county's department of children and family services.

"If a kid has a broken leg, and parents say he doesn't need treatment, that's neglect," said Marlene Wong, the district's director of mental health. "Mental illness is just as real as epilepsy or diabetes."

"Parents have abdicated responsibility," added Ms. Grenados. "The school has to pick up the ball."

Ms. Grenados said she's grateful that once she has identified suicidal or depressed students, she has several places to send them for ongoing help. In addition to referring them to a psychiatric ward, she can sign them up for psychological counseling at a public or private clinic.

But Ms. Grenados also has an option none of her counterparts in other school districts have: a professionally staffed mental health facility operated exclusively for district children.

The nation's only child psychiatric clinic run by a school system is housed in a bungalow classroom shaded by eucalyptus trees in Los Angeles' San Fernando Valley. In a warren of cozy rooms, eleven psychologists, psychiatrists, and social workers counsel district students five days a week.

Students pay nothing for the service, though the district collects reimbursements for students eligible for Medicaid.

With the added help of fifty interns—graduate students in psychology from UCLA and the University of Southern California—the clinic resembles a university health center. It serves seventy patients a day for problems ranging from post-traumatic stress disorder to anger management.

The clinic operates in large part because of a cost-sharing arrangement in which Los Angeles County agreed to provide half the clinic's $1.2 million annual budget. The remainder of the revenue to run the facility comes from reimbursements from Medicaid, for which half the clinic's patients are eligible.

But whether homeless or a millionaire's child, any student gets served, said Gil Palacio, one of the clinic's coordinators. "We take anyone regardless of money," he said.

Despite the district's financial investments, Ms. Wong, the mental health director, said even more must be done to help children in the earliest grades. The seeds of suicide germinate early; psychologists, she said, are able to detect whether children are emotionally troubled as early as pre-school.

"When it's a very bumpy road," she said, "we can bring children back to learning quicker if we start early."

A Safe Place

At City as School in Manhattan* one afternoon in 1999, a crew of about twenty high school students squeezed into a circle of plastic chairs already too small for them. The high-speed chatter—about weekend plans and homework—nearly drowned out the urban din of car horns and pedestrian traffic outside. Half the students in this weekly gender-discussion class are heterosexual, a third are gay or lesbian, and the rest are still in search of a label.

For an hour and a half, these urban adolescents unabashedly delved into whatever topics popped into their heads: sexism, contraception, drug use, depression. Students have even recounted the disturbing details of their suicide attempts to the class. This day's topic was a perennial problem: homophobia.

Alex, an eighteen-year-old who wears a dog collar and lip ring, took the floor to recite a litany of abuse he has suffered. "People call me 'fag', 'queer', 'cocksucker,' " the tall, striking teen declared, as other students nodded knowingly.

Michael Perelman, a charismatic teacher at City as School who helped found this gender discussion group, says the class is one way to get students talking about their prejudices, their fears, and their dreams. Though this class was

---

* EDITOR'S NOTE: At their request, the names of the students at City as School have been changed. All other names are real.

never conceived as a suicide prevention course, it is one. Perelman has personally thwarted several students' suicide attempts over the years. "If they feel they are going to do themselves in, they come to me, and I march them to the counselor's office and we take them to the hospital. That's happened three or four times," said Mr. Perelman.

Gay teenagers are five times more likely to attempt suicide than their straight peers. Gay and lesbian teenagers "grow up feeling they have to hide from everybody. They are rejected and abused by family. They feel unloved," Mr. Perelman said. "This is a place where hope exists for their future."

Winning school approval to earn credit for such a group was far from simple. New York State school officials scrutinize every course that's offered in every school. Mr. Perelman said they purposely called it a "gender discussion" group because some administrators, though supportive of efforts to help gay students, were afraid that district leaders would perceive the session as promoting homosexuality. "We are not telling kids what they are in here," Mr. Perelman said. "We are letting kids tell us what they are."

Kevin Jennings, the director of New York City-based GLSEN, devoted to eradicating antihomosexual attitudes and harassment in schools, said that such discussion groups and more formal gay-straight alliances are critical to making schools a more welcoming place for all students.

Gay-straight alliances are cropping up not just in big cities but also in suburbs and rural areas from Maine to Washington State. Through its network of 15,000 members in eighty-five communities, GLSEN helped increase the number of such clubs from half a dozen in 1990 to more than 600 a decade later.

Mr. Jennings also urges teachers to confront prejudice against gay and lesbian students by integrating positive images of homosexuals into their lesson plans. A former history teacher, Mr. Jennings argues that students ought to be taught about the murder of Matthew Shepard—the gay University of Wyoming student who was battered, tied to a fence, and left to die in 1998—alongside units on the lynchings of black men.

Teaching tolerance ultimately helps protect all students, regardless of their sexual orientation, he added. In a majority of school shootings in 1997 and 1998, antigay harassment was a factor, even when the target of ridicule was heterosexual, several news reports showed. Michael Carneal, age fourteen, went on his school shooting spree in December 1997 in West Paducah, Kentucky, a few weeks after a student newspaper article labeled him gay. Though clearly upset, the boy—who was straight—told his mother he didn't want to make a fuss. The next week, three girls, including the girl who wrote the article, were dead.

Many critics argue strongly, however, that America's classrooms are inappropriate venues to discuss gender, sexuality, or homosexual issues.

"What they call teaching tolerance, we call advocating homosexuality, and we believe homosexuality is morally wrong," said Peter LaBarbera, a senior policy analyst at the Family Research Council, a Washington, D.C.-based research and advocacy group.

Mr. LaBarbera also said he objects to a group's being singled out for special attention in schools. "We think it's terribly wrong when any child is hurt or abused, but there are a lot of groups that get picked on, like skinny boys and fat girls, and we don't have specific policies for them," he said.

Some state leaders agree. In 1996, the Utah legislature took the unprecedented step of barring all extracurricular clubs at schools rather than allowing alliances of gay and straight students to form and meet. Then, in 1999, Oregon groups circulated petitions to put an initiative on the ballot that would prohibit discussion of lesbian and gay issues in schools.

Despite such opposition, gay and lesbian advocacy groups point to several legislative victories. Since GLSEN was founded in 1994, Massachusetts, Wisconsin, Connecticut, and California have enacted laws that prohibit discrimination or harassment against students based on their sexual orientation. Several court decisions also have made it more costly for public schools to ignore antigay harassment.

In 1996, a federal district court ruled that the 2,400-student Ashland, Wisconsin, school district's failure to discipline a student who repeatedly beat a gay student had violated the equal protection clause of the U.S. Constitution. The district was ordered to pay the student, Jamie S. Nabozny, $900,000.

Some gay-rights advocates contend that until antidiscrimination laws apply to gay students in every school, separate institutions ought to be available for homosexual teenagers. In the same spirit in which historically black colleges were founded to serve African-American students, a New York City educator and psychologist established the Harvey Milk School—named after the slain San Francisco city supervisor and gay-rights activist—fifteen years ago to serve the educational needs of gay youths.

Christian Luckie was sixteen when he transferred to the school in 1997, after a campaign of antigay harassment by other students compelled his parents to find a different learning environment for him.

"It was hard to think, 'Am I going to get cut or burned today?' and then try to concentrate on my grades at the same time," the teenager said matter-of-factly. "Before I came here, I was going to drop out. This school was like winning the lottery."

But people who work with gay youths say that even if those students attend the most welcoming school, gay teenagers also need a safe place to be after school, particularly if they feel ostracized at home.

The Gay and Lesbian Community Center, a six-story converted warehouse, is a gathering spot for more than 300 gay and lesbian teenagers in New York City. On one fall afternoon in 1999, a small contingent of teenagers was busy composing first-person articles for the center's snappy newsmagazine, *Out Youth*. Another group was squeezed into the small computer lab, working on homework.

Bridget Hughes, who runs the center's youth programs, said newcomers to the center are often wary of adults. Many are runaways or homeless, and some have harrowing stories of prostitution or taking refuge with adults who have then exploited them for sex.

Ms. Hughes said she keeps a list of referral agencies handy to consult when a suicidal youth needs professional psychological help, medical attention, or just a safe place to bunk for the night.

"Sometimes, the kids circle the building five times to decide if they want to come in. But then they calm down when they see I don't have horns and this isn't a dungeon," said Ms. Hughes, who takes pride in the transforming effect the center seems to have on gay teenagers. "It only takes a few months from a kid thinking their life is over to being somebody who is reaching out to take care of somebody else."

EMPATHY 101

Squinting into the lunch-hour sunshine, Jackie Garcia scans the vast, blacktop playground for signs of altercations. Spotting a scuffle between a pair of second graders playing kickball, Jackie, age eleven, bounds toward them, her bright-orange slicker, emblazoned with the title "Conflict Manager," flapping as she runs.

"Okay, what happened?" she quizzes the seven-year-olds, who in turn begin mumbling exaggerated tales of wrongs. After eliciting promises that the children will cease their pushing and name-calling, the fifth grader marks their names on her clipboard. The young combatants shake hands and resume their game as Jackie dashes to the water fountain to mediate another schoolyard melee.

Beginning in kindergarten, students at Elizabeth Learning Center in Los Angeles, California, learn how to play nice.

Ever since a series of multiple-victim shootings erupted at schools across the country in the 1990s, the American public has worried that schools are hazardous places where peer rivalries fester and plots to wreak violence play out under administrators' noses. But Elizabeth Learning Center might as well post a sign out front saying, "Columbine couldn't happen here."

Besides the conflict-resolution patrols, the tidy public school in Cudahy, deep in the Los Angeles barrio, is a virtual shopping mall of wellness programs, packed with social services a student in trouble might need: a full-time school psychologist, a team of five counselors, a physician-staffed medical clinic, speech therapists, individual tutoring, and adult education classes for neighborhood residents.

"There's a family feeling here," Emilio Vasquez, the perpetually smiling principal, said of the 3,000-student K-12 school he calls his "big red schoolhouse."

This experiment in changing a school's climate started five years ago in the offices of Howard Adelman, the UCLA psychologist who operates a laboratory of sorts for nurturing schools. Through a three-year, multimillion-dollar grant, the school was reorganized to address the emotional needs of children and their families.

The aim was to use Elizabeth Learning Center to test Mr. Adelman's experimental ideas. If the children thrived academically and emotionally when exposed to an array of services, then more schools like it could be coaxed to grow.

"This isn't some mindless self-esteem stuff," Mr. Adelman said. "It's about programmatic restructuring of schools to remove barriers to learning."

Mr. Adelman chose the school because the students here face every barrier in the book—malnutrition, asthma, learning disabilities, chaotic home lives.

Students' parents, mostly immigrant families from Mexico, Puerto Rico, and El Salvador, are so poor that a single apartment often houses three families. The average per capita income is $9,000 a year—one of the lowest in the nation—making every student eligible for the federal free and reduced-price meals program.

Drive-by shootings are a common menace in Cudahy, a city the Los Angeles Police Department says has one of the highest murder rates in Los Angeles County. More than fifteen Latino gangs patrol the filthy, narrow streets at night, forcing most residents to remain in their homes after sunset to avoid gunfire. So routine is the violence here that students don't seem to flinch if they hear the crackle of flying bullets on their way home from school. To many residents, Elizabeth Learning Center's fenced-in campus is a refuge in a war zone.

The place looks like other schools, with its uniformed children playing and laughing in the California sun at recess. But a closer look reveals research-tested education reform experiments running in virtually every corner.

In 1995, what was then a middle school became the K–12 Elizabeth Learning Center, containing three schools that work as cohesive units. The transition grades between elementary, middle, and high school are often the periods when many students become discipline problems and their grades tend to decline. Having three schools in one eliminates the need to adjust to a new environment, Mr. Vasquez, the principal, said.

"The kids aren't changing anything. It's the same campus, same teachers, same lunch tables," he said. "There are no new territories to establish, nothing to prove, and they don't have all this new bravado."

Just in case, the school trains older "peer leaders" to give the fifth and eighth grade students any transition assistance—new pencils, notebooks, a companion at lunchtime—they may require.

Another hallmark of the New American Schools reform model being replicated at Elizabeth Learning Center is small class sizes. Most teachers have between fifteen and twenty students. Aside from the education benefits of more personalized instruction, "It's easier to let your feelings out in small settings," said Richard Rusiecki, one of the school's three psychologists.

A critical part of creating a kinder, gentler school is picking the right people.

"You can't get somebody who doesn't work well with other people, or you're dead," Mr. Vasquez said. This is a place where everyone from the groundskeeper to the principal is enlisted as an emotional custodian.

On one Monday morning in the fall of 1999, the "learning supports" committee gathered around a conference table for its weekly meeting to share information about students' problems and to organize a timely, coordinated response. Made up of school personnel from different departments, the team governs all school business from curriculum selection and facilities maintenance to budget and parental involvement.

At another fall 1999 meeting, two special education teachers, a school psychologist, two counselors, a nurse, and a speech therapist charged with safeguarding the mental health of students slowly plowed through the week's case files.

First was Julio, a first grader with a serious speech impediment and apparent hearing loss. He needs to return to kindergarten and go to language training, the committee members all agreed. The nurse said she would get him to a doctor to rule out an ear infection.

Next on the list was Erica, a belligerent kindergartner who would strike her teacher and wouldn't sit still in class. The teacher and counselor speculated on a diagnosis. Attention deficit hyperactivity disorder? Emotional trauma? One of them wrote a note: "Call the mother. Psychiatric exam needed."

A governing principle at Elizabeth Learning Center is regular, scheduled communication involving all the staff members who touch the life of each child in the school. Mental health experts say that many schools miss warning signs of impending criminal or self-destructive behavior because staff don't share information with the teacher in the next classroom, let alone the school nurse.

While hardly foolproof, coordinating data among multiple points of contact makes it harder for students' problems to fall through the cracks at Elizabeth, Mr. Rusiecki, the school psychologist, said.

Mr. Rusiecki recalls one eighteen-year-old senior who wrote a note in class saying, "I don't want to live because I'm a disappointment to my father." As soon as the boy's teacher retrieved the note, the teacher met with Mr. Rusiecki, who referred the senior that day to a mental health clinic two miles from the school. The boy and his father went to counseling.

With the idea that serving the community's need for improved education and psychological services ultimately will benefit students, the school sacrificed three bungalow classrooms to operate a family center.

The more than sixty parent volunteers, mostly women, who staff the center perform a myriad of tasks, such as arranging counseling appointments for students, aiding teachers, and helping patrol the schoolyard. But the parents are also eligible for services for themselves.

In one of the classrooms, more than 700 parents stream in from 9 A.M. to 8:30 P.M. Monday through Thurs-

day for classes in areas such as computer use, aerobics, knit-
ting, citizenship, and those needed to earn a high school
equivalency diploma, or GED.

Most of the parents don't have a diploma, and research
has shown that improving a parent's English skills can help
improve children's academic achievement. To encourage
attendance, the center offers a day-care center next door
that is also staffed by parent volunteers.

The school also offers individual psychological counseling for parents who themselves are in crisis.

Maria Elena Gonzalez remembers when she came into
the Family Center a few years ago, utterly distraught about
her daughter, Susan, then in high school. The fifteen-year-
old had nearly died from an overdose of Tylenol and alcohol after her boyfriend was shot during a gang battle in the
neighborhood. The girl was hospitalized and released but
had become a heavy user of cocaine, marijuana, and LSD.
Ms. Gonzalez, who couldn't afford a private-practice psychologist, went to the school's professional staff for advice.

"The counselor helped me figure out how to talk to my
daughter, and now she's doing okay," Ms. Gonzalez said.

Emi Elizondo, the director of the Family Center, said
the full-service school concept often means reaching into
areas that usually are reserved for other public institutions.

Like many school improvement efforts, the Elizabeth
Learning Center experiment isn't cheap. The school costs $8
million a year to run, from teachers' salaries to clinic supplies to custodial mops. Besides money from the school district and the start-up grant, the school has received funding
from several foundations.

School leaders have found creative ways to cut
expenses. For one thing, the parent volunteers who together

log more than 1,000 hours a month save the school nearly $10,000 a month.

No sure statistical barometers measure how the school climate has changed since the new organization was first adopted, but the results are encouraging.

Student suspensions—an average of five a week—are down from dozens a day and are now mostly for fighting or dress-code infractions rather than weapons possession or assault. Besides feeling safer, students here are less apt to be self-destructive than their counterparts at other schools.

Neighboring Bell High School averaged two suicide attempts per week in the 1990s. Since Elizabeth Learning Center opened, not a single student has taken his or her life and there have been no known attempts. At the same time, the school's test scores have inched up: In 1996, Elizabeth students scored in the sixteenth percentile on state tests; in 1999, they rose to the twentieth.

Kids stay in school: The dropout rate hovers near 2 percent, and the graduation rate—at 95 percent in 2000—is double that of the neighboring schools.

Mr. Vasquez says that the larger life lessons taught at his school are as valuable a part of the curriculum as calculus and biology.

Around 7:30 A.M. on a chilly fall day in 1999, a crew of fifty fourth and fifth graders plunked down on long plastic tables for their weekly conflict-resolution class before heading to homeroom.

Jackie Garcia, donning her orange vest at a head table with a half-dozen other "conflict managers," listened attentively as school counselor Gary Burbank went over the basic points of mediating a playground scuffle: Don't take sides or interrupt, listen actively, and make eye contact.

"The byword here is empathy," Mr. Burbank told the children. "Does anyone remember that word? We try to understand how they feel and to understand why they are so unhappy."

CONCLUSION

THE DAY BEFORE I set out to write this conclusion, a 12-year-old boy in a suburb of Washington, D.C., hung himself in the basement of his home. A colleague of mine who is a neighbor of the family told me the news as we were fetching our morning coffee in the newsroom kitchen.

What struck me about the horrific event was its proximity. I have a dear friend whose husband committed suicide in his twenties. But I've never known, before I began the research for this book, a teenager who'd taken his or her own life.

While suicide among the young is still relatively rare, it is also true that few people don't know someone who knows some child who has done it—or at least made an attempt. Perhaps it was a classmate of their son or daughter, a distant cousin, or a friend's child. Three degrees of separation. Maybe four or five.

Few communities are spared the jolt of a teenager's death because not in recent memory have the young chosen to die at such alarming rates. Youth suicide has tripled since

1960, and now ranks as the third leading cause of death for teens.

As I detailed in this book, children are far more beleaguered and far less supported today than in years past. Even though many children may live in families that are better off financially, life has become increasingly chaotic for many young people. Parents in most income brackets work more hours than they did thirty years ago, and as a result children are spending more time alone after school. More teenagers engage in more solitary activities like watching television or surfing the Web. One survey showed that kids spend more hours per week with inanimate electronic devices like video games than they do with their parents.

Not only has the home environment become more isolating for children today, it has also become more hazardous. Kids are more likely to be beaten or witness abuse than they did several decades ago. More young people are drinking alcohol and using drugs like methamphetamines now than they did in the 1960s. Children are having sex at much younger ages than they did in the past. In 1988, 56 percent of girls and 73 percent of boys had sex before their 18th birthday. In 1958, 27 percent of girls and 55 percent of boys had sex by the time they turned 18.

The school environment in the last few decades has also become increasingly violent. Many teenagers bring their unexpressed grief to school and inflict punishments on their classmates. By most estimates, bullying is on the rise. Students are more likely to be victimized if they are in a minority group, and especially if they are gay.

Academic pressures add to children's stress. Most students, especially the high achievers, say they feel more pressured than ever as most states have adopted new higher standards that children must meet in order to graduate. Also, there is greater competition than ever before for students to get into college.

Even though this unflattering image of America's youth is backed by solid statistics, people often fail to acknowledge it. Perhaps that is simply a collective act of denial. But just because many adults may be faring well in today's booming economy, that doesn't mean their children are equally elated. By nearly every objective measure, children today seem to be more off-kilter and unbalanced than ever. Extra money, toys and games don't exempt any child in any family from feeling lonely and wounded or scared. And school officials are often so overwhelmed by getting children up to speed academically they rarely take the time to check students' emotional health.

For children, though, ignoring their own crushing heartache is not so simple. More and more children who find it difficult to cope see committing suicide as their one escape. It seems to be the only clear solution to this bewildering isolation they feel on a daily basis. The tragedy is that many children are too young to know their decision is final. And if they do know what they are doing, many teenagers camouflage their problems from their parents and even their friends until it's too late.

To be sure, most researchers agree that the most direct way to reduce the number of teenagers who take their own lives would be to eliminate the most popular means of self-destruction. More effective gun control policies, including trigger locks, could save many lives as more than half of all people in the United States who commit suicide use a firearm.

However, a lasting solution to preventing suicide has to go deeper than clamping locks on every gun in circulation or installing elaborate safety devices on new firearms sold. We have looked at a variety of prevention measures in this book, including quick school presentations on suicide and inexpensive mail-order suicide prevention kits. Experts argue that superficial solutions won't work to solve these problems. Those programs that confront children's angst and anger directly, offer them a safe and supportive environment, and receive ample financial support tend to yield the most promising results. Researchers argue that the best way for society to attack this problem is by striking on all fronts: Find ways to reduce child abuse and family violence, facilitate ways for parents to spend more time with their children, make schools more tolerant and less hostile. Basically, it's about making the world a little more hospitable for kids.

While not every one of these prevention strategies has to have a dollar attached to it, the reluctance on the part of the public and political leaders to invest more in proven prevention strategies is troubling to many in the field. While teenage suicide rates tripled, funding for mental health services in schools has flatlined. Politicians and community leaders have failed to address the seriousness of the problem even though Surgeon General David Satcher calls suicide one of the most serious public health epidemics we face today.

Ultimately there needs to be a cultural shift to change the status quo of thousands of teen suicides a year. But until that occurs, parents, schools, and students can have an impact in many small but important ways.

Parents can elect to have more time alone with their children. They can stay better connected to their children's teachers and friends, which can help them understand their elusive teenager's mental state. More than 70 percent of the time, a suicide victim told someone beforehand they were going to do it. If children feel close to their parents, they may feel disposed to reveal such a confidence. Parents can also quiz their children about homework burdens and help them get tutoring or additional help if they need it. Parents can enroll their children in community groups like Big Brothers and Big Sisters. A study of the nationwide group found that, along with better grades, children who participate in community groups, tend to be less likely to be depressed than other children. Parents can also be tolerant if their child tells them they are gay or lesbian. Single, divorced, or married parents can get counseling for themselves if they are having problems in their relationships so that the child isn't put in the position of referee.

And lastly, parents whose children exhibit severe emotional mood swings might get them psychological counseling. Early diagnosis of mental illness can significantly cut the suicide rate among teens, who, as a population, tend to be the least likely to visit a doctor.

Schools, for their part, can start teaching children to play nice from kindergarten forward. Through tough discipline policies, schools can teach students how not to be bullies in the classroom and in the lunchroom. In this book, I point to exemplary conflict resolution and anger management courses which teach kids how to stop other kids from fighting and impose strict codes of conduct from the day students set foot on the playground. Bullies in these schools are dealt with harshly and must answer to the principal.

Schools who also help children succeed academically can strengthen children's overall outlook on life. For example, children with learning disabilities like dyslexia are more at risk for depression and suicide than other children. Simply getting them help could keep them from sinking into an emotional funk. Some districts, like those I mentioned in the book, have found that hiring more mental health workers to treat children on site helps tremendously. School psychologists and counselors are uniquely equipped to identify teenagers in that window of time after they've thought about killing themselves but before they've actually made an attempt. Finally, schools might have a method for teens to anonymously report their friends' suicidal thoughts and should respond quickly by calling the parents as soon as they are aware of a problem. Many schools already have these policies on the books but don't enforce them.

Many believe that the answer to preventing youth suicide lies in removing the desire to die. In this regard, students are in a unique position to talk their friends down from the brink. Students need to be extra alert if their friends say anything particularly morose, especially if it's out of character. A suicide note in class ought to be turned into a teacher, and a cryptic statement about ending it all should never be taken as idle chatter. Students need to know its OK to tell someone and that they can break their friends' confidence if it means saving their friends' life.

Students can also work as a team and with teachers to create a more harmonious school environment. The philosophy that a peaceful solution is possible and that all conflicts can be resolved can permeate a school campus when enough students embrace it. Bullies may not be ejected from these schools altogether, but they can be made to look less cool, which is the ultimate slight.

Though its still unclear why the 12-year-old boy in suburban Washington decided to kill himself this year, his death has already galvanized the community around him. Parents, communities, students, schools, and governments at all levels ultimately have the power to create a safer world for the youngest and most vulnerable among us. My hope is this book will help people face this deep and complex problem and find some way, whether momentous or modest, that they can be part of a meaningful solution.

APPENDICES

APPENDIX 1. Method of Suicide in the Age Group 10 to 19, by Gender, 1993–1997.

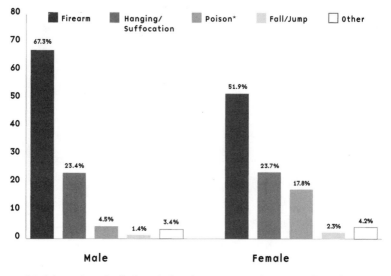

* Includes overdoses of medication and other substances. *NOTE: Totals may not equal 100% due to rounding.*

SOURCE: U.S. Centers for Disease Control and Prevention

APPENDIX 2.   Suicide Rates Among Black Youth and White Youth, 1980–1995.

Although blacks historically have had a lower suicide rate than whites, the gap has narrowed significantly in the past two decades. The suicide rate for black 10- to 19-year-olds increased from 2.1 per 100,000 population in 1980 to 4.5 per 100,000 by 1995. The rate for white youths increased from 5.4 in 1980 to 6.4 in 1995

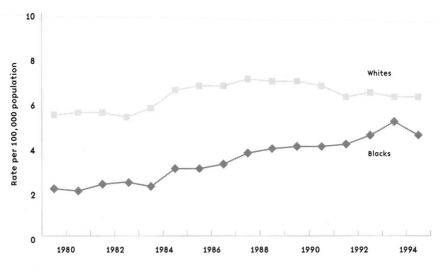

SOURCE: U.S. Centers for Disease Control and Prevention

APPENDIX 3. Total Expenditures by U.S. Mental Health Groups, 1969–1994.

Measured in current dollars, total expenditures by mental-health groups in the United States increased from $3.3 billion in 1969 to $33.1 billion in 1994. That means that inflation accounts for 95 percent of the increase, while spending power by mental-health organizations increased only 5 percent.

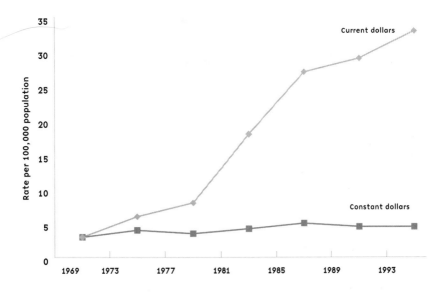

SOURCE: U.S. Department of Health and Human Services

APPENDIX 4. Where Children Go for Mental Health Services.

Each year, an estimated 21 percent of children are diagnosed with mental or addictive disorders and seek treatment. More than half of those childen receive mental-health services at school.

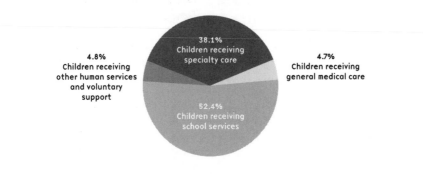

SOURCE: "Mental Health: A Report of the Surgeon General," U.S. Department of Health and Human Services

APPENDIX 5. Average Youth Suicide Rates per 100,000
Population, by Region and State, 1994–1997.

The Western states, especially the region that flanks the long spine of the Rocky
Mountains—Montana, Nevada, Colorado, and Utah—consistently have among the
highest percentages of teenage suicides in the country. The map below shows an
average of state-by-state suicide rates for 1994–97, calculated per 100,000
youths ages 10 to 19. Experts at the U.S. Centers for Disease Control and
Prevention say one reason for the high rates in the Western half of the country
is that residents of prairie and mountain states are more socially isolated. Some
also have speculated that the rate is higher because those with a pioneering
spirit who migrate West may be disappointed when they arrive at their
destinations and their high expectations aren't met. If depression strikes,
mental-health care tends to be harder to access in those regions. Less populated
states also tend to have fewer community institutions such as parks and
recreational activities to bring far-flung people together. Higher suicide rates
may also be connected to a larger number of firearms in circulation per capita in
the West and the South. Individual states are ranked below, beginning with
Alaska, the state with the highest teenage suicide rate.

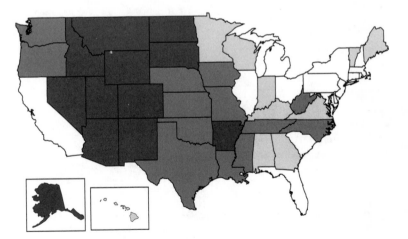

■ 8.6 to 14.7 suicides per 100,000 youths   ▨ 5.7 to 6.3 suicides per 100,000 youths

■ 8.3 to 8.6 suicides per 100,000 youths   □ 2.7 to 5.7 suicides per 100,000 youths

SOURCE: U.S. Centers for Disease Control and Prevention

APPENDIX 6. Suicide Warning Signs

Having knowledge of suicide warning signs is the first step in being able to help an adolescent in need. Contrary to common belief, about 80 percent of those who attempt suicide do exhibit signs. Several of these signs together may indicate it's time to talk openly with the individual you are concerned about.

It is important to remember, however, that even healthy teens exhibit some of these signs from time to time. No one single sign is a sure indicator of suicide. Look for a pattern and trust your instincts!

VERBAL

Direct statements like the following need immediate attention:

"I want to die"

"I don't want to live anymore"

"Life sucks and I want to get out"

"I hate myself"

Indirect statements can also give clues:

"I want to go to sleep and never wake up"

"They'll be sorry when I'm gone"

"Soon the pain will be over"

BEHAVIORAL

Lack of energy

Acting bored or disinterested

Tearful sadness

Difficulty concentrating or making decisions

Silent or withdrawn

Angry and destructive

Less interest in usual activities

Giving away prized possessions

Confusion

Dwelling on death in creative activities such as music, poetry and drawing

Difficulty sleeping or changing sleep patterns

Increased thrill seeking and risky behaviors

Increased use of drugs and alcohol

Change in appearance and cleanliness

Change in appetite or eating habits

Poor school performance

ENVIRONMENTAL

Previous suicide attempts by a family member or friend

Problems at school

Family violence

Sexual abuse

Major family change

The most vulnerable times for youth suicides are during "rites of passage," including graduation, anniversaries and birthdays. Many teens also commit suicide a short interval after a disciplinary crisis or after a rejection or humiliation.

Issues surrounding homosexuality are worth special notice. Research has shown that 30 percent of all completed youth suicides are related to issues of sexual identity.

Gun safety is also a crucial precaution that every gun owner should practice. Statistics show that the risk of suicide is five times greater if there's a gun in the home. Basic safety includes locking the guns and ammunition in separate containers—Empty It Out & Lock It Up!

SOURCE: *Warning Signs* taken from a presentation developed by Youth Crisis Stabilization Program, Community Health and Counseling Services, Bangor, Maine.

INDEX